IMAGES
of America

CHESTER

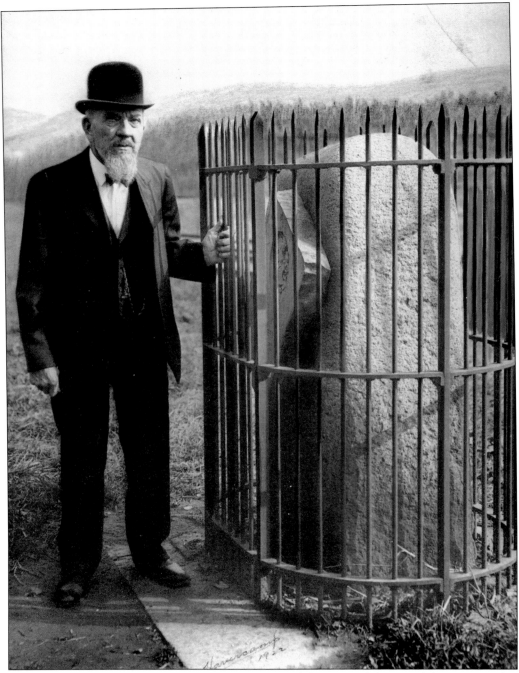

Members of the Historical Society of Pennsylvania and the Penn Club erected the Penn Marker in 1882. Constructed of granite, it is about five feet tall and three feet by two feet wide at the base, weighing over two tons. The marble tablet reads, "This stone marks the spot where William Penn landed October 28 and 29, 1682."

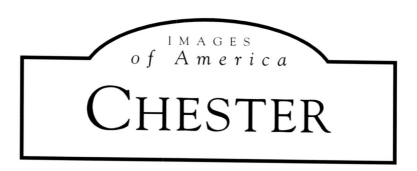

IMAGES
of America

CHESTER

Chester Historical
Preservation Committee

ARCADIA
PUBLISHING

Published by Arcadia Publishing
Charleston, South Carolina

Printed in the Unites States of America

Library of Congress Catalog Card Number: 2004108755

For all general information contact Arcadia Publishing at:
Telephone 843-853-2070
Fax 843-853-0044
E-mail sales@arcadiapublishing.com
For customer service and orders:
Toll-Free 1-888-313-2665

Visit us on the Internet at www.arcadiapublishing.com

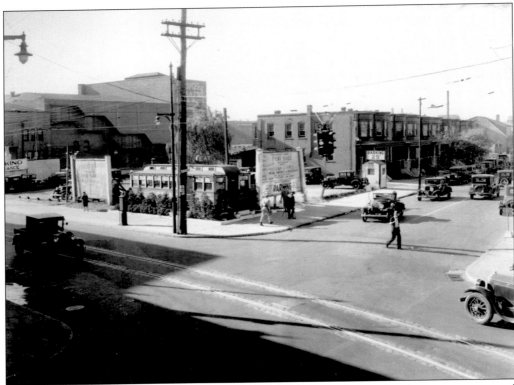

The Chester Diner, seen in this 1930s photograph, was one of many local restaurants around Chester where residents could grab a cup of coffee and a luncheon special on a work day.

CONTENTS

ACKNOWLEDGMENTS

The Chester Historical Preservation Committee was incorporated in 1983 to preserve and educate the people of this area about the historic importance of Chester. Our dedicated members and the community assisted with the collection of photographs and research for this project. We especially want to thank those who attended our photograph-scanning sessions. The photographs that the public provided greatly increased our Chester archives.

The Chester Friends Meeting graciously allowed us the space to hold our meetings and scanning sessions.

We would also like to offer special thanks to the Delaware County Historical Society for the use of their extensive collection of Chester photographs. Mary Anne Jeavons and the library staff were most helpful in locating Chester materials for the book.

Without the dedication and computer skills of Bob Myers, this book would not have been published. He spent many long hours scanning and editing the photographs. His wife, Mary Margaret, assisted Bob with the production of the book.

Dave Andrews, a former resident of Chester, wrote the introduction. Also many thanks to Marianne Hampton, as her knowledge of Chester was invaluable.

Last but certainly not least, many thanks to the Chester Historical Preservation Committee members who spent endless hours in the preparation of this book. Members include Dave Guleke (president), Carol Fireng (vice president), Doris Vermeychuk (secretary), Helen Wright, Bob and Mary Myers, Dan Vermeychuk, Andy Maginnis, and Ed Broadfield.

For information about events and projects of the Chester Historical Preservation Committee, visit our Web site www.delcohistory.org/chester.

INTRODUCTION

Before Europeans came to this area, the Lenni Lenape occupied the basin of the Delaware River. Gov. Johan Printz, the first native-born Swede to lead the New Sweden Colony, moved his capital to Tinicum. The Swedish crown granted the greater part of the land from what is now the Crozer-Chester Hospital to the Delaware River between Chester Creek and Ridley Creek to Joran Kyn, who grew tobacco. The area was called Upland after a province in Sweden (Uppland). The colony changed control from Sweden to the Dutch, and finally to the English, but Armgalo Papegoya, daughter of Governor Printz, stayed in the colony to handle property belonging to her father. In 1675, she sold her home on the Delaware River below Chester Creek to Robert Wade, the first Quaker to reside in Upland.

In 1681, William Penn petitioned the duke of York for a colony in America for persecuted Quakers. The petition was granted, and Penn's cousin, William Markham (deputy governor), set up Pennsylvania's seat of government in Upland. The following year, William Penn first landed in Upland, Pennsylvania, on the ship *Welcome*, where he stayed in the home of Robert Wade. The first assembly was held in Upland and later moved to Philadelphia. In 1701, Penn's Charter of Privileges Guaranteeing Freedom of Religion was granted by the British crown, and Chester was incorporated as a borough. In 1724, the Colonial Court House (the oldest public building in continuous use in the United States) was built and opened. There was much activity surrounding the American Revolution in Chester. "Mad" Anthony Wayne made his headquarters at the courthouse. After the Battle of Brandywine, the American army straggled into Chester, where Washington wrote the only account of the battle and Lafayette had his wound treated. Later, Lord Cornwallis used Chester as a point of debarkation for an attack in New Jersey. Eighty British ships lay in the river off Chester. Washington later passed through Chester on the way to Yorktown to defeat and capture Cornwallis.

In 1789, Delaware County was created, separating it from Chester County, and Chester was named the county seat. During June, July, and August 1790, John Fitch ran a steamboat carrying freight between Wilmington, Chester, and Philadelphia—nearly 17 years before Robert Fulton made his successful venture on the Hudson River. In 1824, General Lafayette was greeted in Chester at the courthouse on his farewell tour of America.

Kitts and Kurlin established a machine shop and foundry on the west side of Edgmont Avenue at Fifth Street in 1837, creating the first manufacturing establishment in Chester. The following year, the Philadelphia, Wilmington and Baltimore Railroad was opened for travel and freight from Wilmington to Philadelphia. It ran along Sixth Street at ground level. This was the beginning of a giant industrialization of Chester. In 1850, the Delaware County seat was moved to Media, and James Campbell bought the old jail and established the Pioneer Mills, the first textile mill in Chester. The Act of Assembly incorporated Chester as a city in 1866, and John Larkin Jr. became the first mayor. The boundaries of the city were complete in 1898, when South Chester Borough was incorporated into the city of Chester. North Chester Borough had already been incorporated into the city of Chester in 1887. Shipbuilding flourished along the Delaware River for the better part of 150 years. The Roach shipyard, located in Chester, built 219 iron vessels over a 36-year period beginning in 1871.

Some of the many industries that grew up in Chester were Scott Paper, Baldt Anchor, Sun Ship, Penn Steel, Ford Motors, Chester Brewery, and Ranger Joe. The motto of the city seemed to have been "What Chester makes makes Chester."

With the development of industry, many ethnic groups were drawn to the city, where they built their own churches and other social institutions. This book will attempt to portray the history of Chester and of its people in their life pursuits.

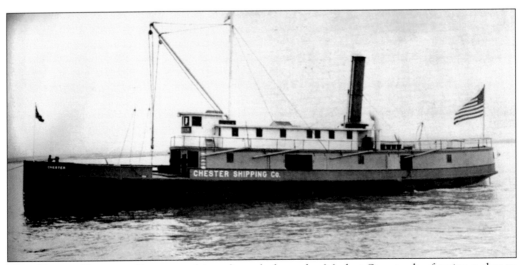

The Chester Shipping Company shipped goods from the Market Street wharf twice a day to Philadelphia 100 years ago.

One

VIEWS OF THE CITY

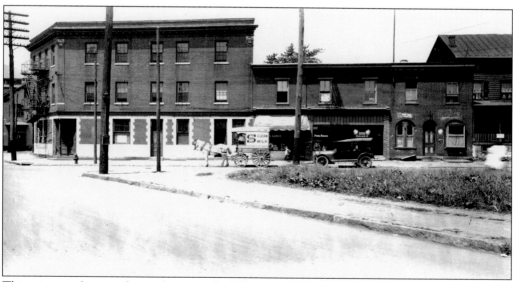

This picture shows a horse-drawn milk-delivery wagon along Morton Avenue above Fifth Street. The Supplee, Will and Jones Dairy was located near the Deshong estate. (DCHS.)

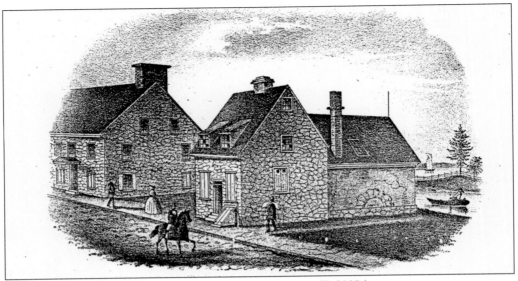

The first Friends meetinghouse in Chester is shown here. (DCHS.)

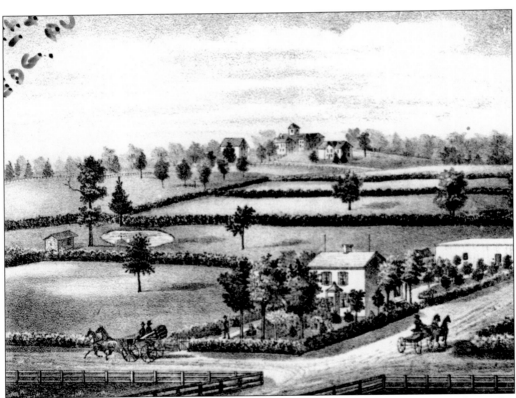

John Walker's farm was located at 24th and Edgemont Streets. Large farms such as this surrounded Chester. (Ella Donlevie.)

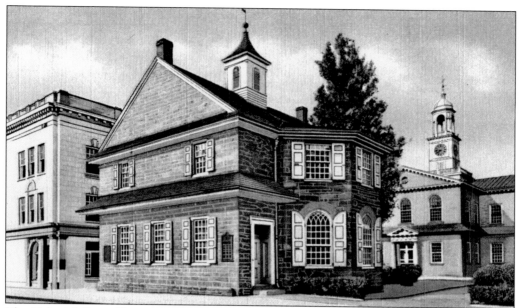

The Colonial Court House, seen here, is one of the oldest government buildings in the country. During Victorian times, the courthouse was altered to reflect the style of the period but was returned to its original state in 1924.

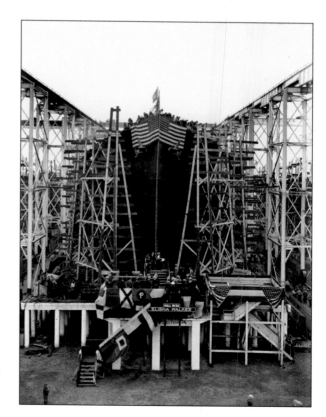

The launching of the *Elisha Walker* is captured at Sun Ship in this photograph from 1920. Shipbuilding is one of the many industries that spawned Chester's growth.

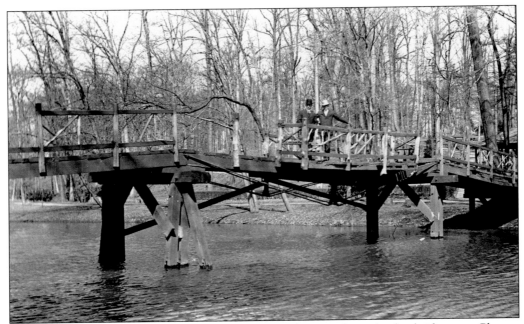

Students of Crozer Theological Seminary pose for a photograph on the footbridge over Chester Creek more than 100 years ago.

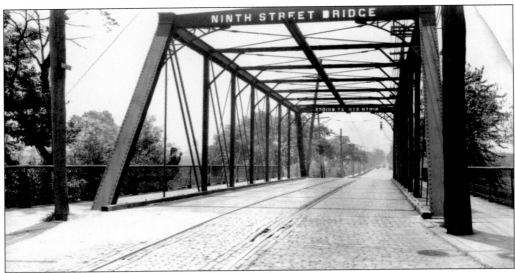

The Ninth Street Bridge was one of the modern bridges that began to make room for motorized traffic in the growing city. (DCHS.)

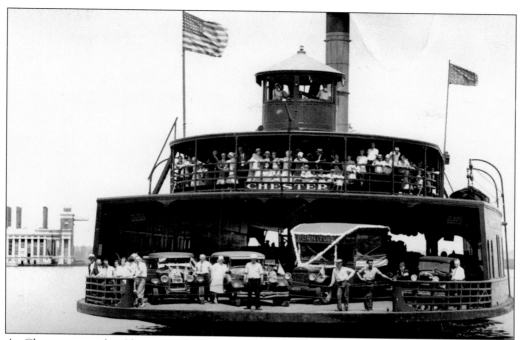

As Chester grew, the Chester Bridgeport Ferry was needed to bring goods and workers into the city. (DCHS.)

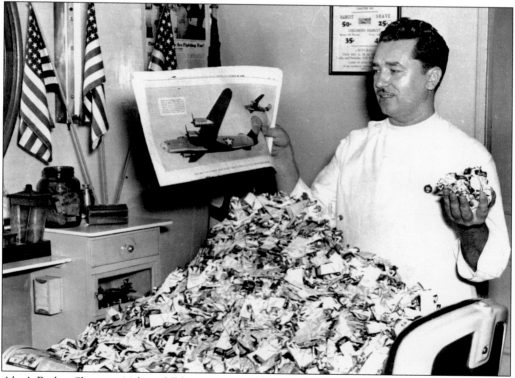

Alex's Barber Shop, at 14th and Edgemont, saved Vitalis tubes for the war effort. (Al Palagruto.)

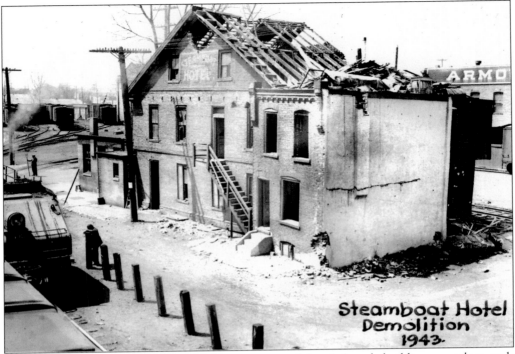

As Chester grew throughout the 20th century, many of the city's early buildings were lost, such as the Steamboat Inn, seen here. (DCHS.)

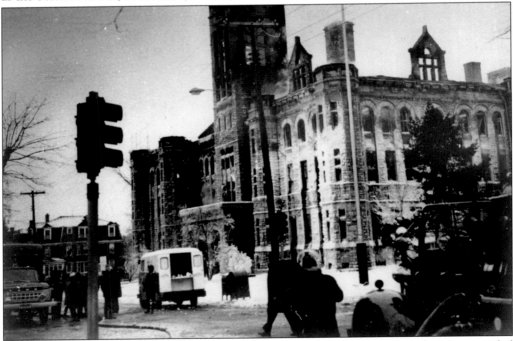

Chester High School was built in 1904. Students from all over Delaware County attended classes here before the building burned in 1968. (DCHS.)

Two

INDUSTRY ON THE DELAWARE

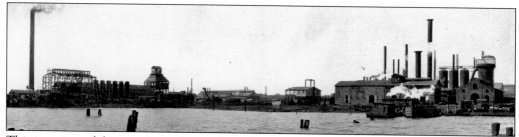

This is a view of the growing industry along the Delaware River in 1903.

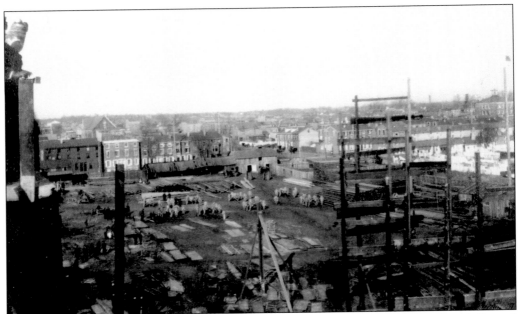

The shipyards of John Roach were purchased in 1871 from Thomas Reamey and Samuel Archibold, who built them in 1859. Among the ships built in the yard were the monitors *Sagamon* and *Lehigh*. By 1874 and under Roach's development, the yard was building the largest merchant ships ever manufactured in America for the Pacific Mail Steamship Company. (DCHS.)

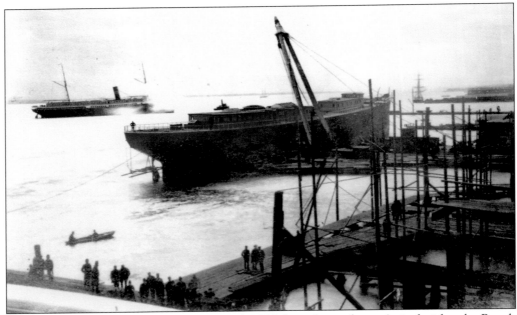

John Roach's shipyard covered 32 acres and 1,200 feet of river front. At its height, the Roach yard employed over 1,500 workers. In 1917, the Harrimans, who had developed the Union Pacific Railroad, bought out his yard. The name was changed to the Chester Shipbuilding Company and later the Merchant's Shipbuilding Company. (DCHS.)

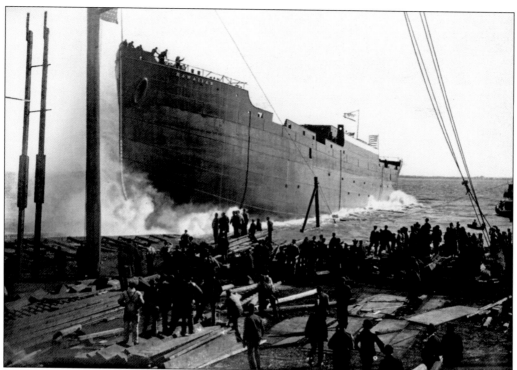

John Roach was a self-made man of legendary ability who began life as an Irish immigrant hod carrier and learned a trade working in a New York foundry. Roach was one of the first shipbuilders to build navy ships under modern contracts, similar to what the navy uses today. (DCHS.)

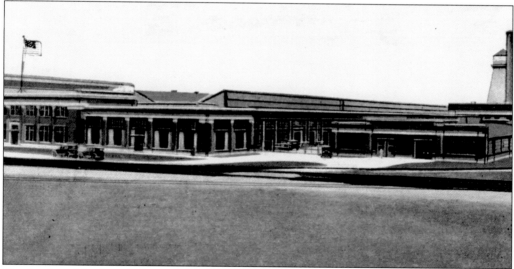

On the site of the Roach shipyard, Ford Motor Company built a plant in Chester that produced cars from 1928 to 1961. The Ford factory was one of the big three industries in Chester that spawned the slogan "What Chester makes makes Chester." The other two factories were Sun Ship and Scott Paper.

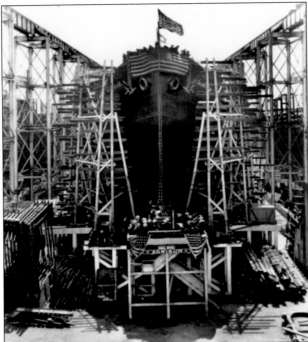

The Sun Shipbuilding Company was started in 1916 and produced tankers and freight ships for private industry, as well as the Victory ships for World War II. The Sun Shipbuilding yard was one of the greatest yards in the building of commercial ships in the nation and the world. The company's last ship, *Westward Venture*, was launched on February 15, 1977.

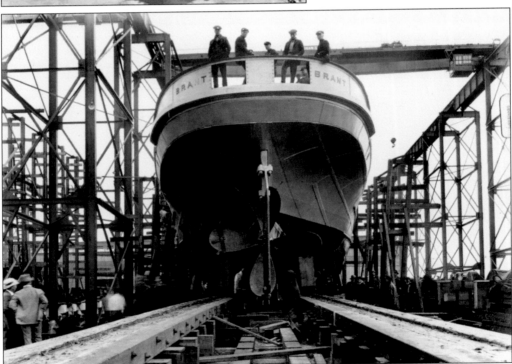

The Sun Shipbuilding Company was an innovator in the construction of ships, and during World War II, the company launched one ship a month. This meant that during the war, the number of ways was increased from 8 to 28.

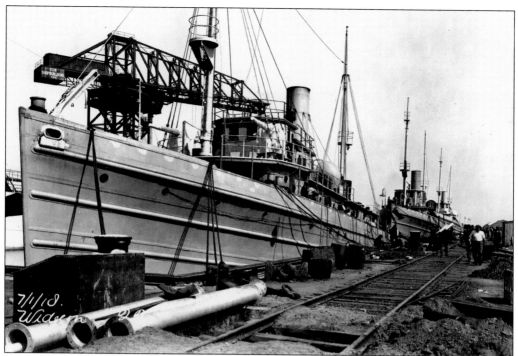

Two of the small gunships, the *Widgeon* and *Teal*, were built by the Sun Shipbuilding Company for the navy during World War I. These ships were among the first 30 built at the yard.

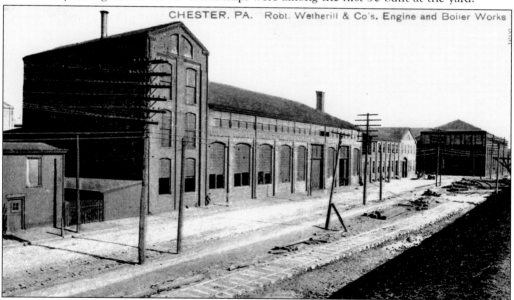

In 1916, the Sun Shipbuilding Company purchased the Wetherill Company for the purpose of building tools for their operation. Robert Wetherill Sr. founded the company in 1871 as Wetherill, Keesey, and Whildey. The following year, Robert formed a partnership with his brother Richard Wetherill, and the name of the firm was changed to Robert Wetherill and Company. Wetherill manufactured the Corliss steam engine.

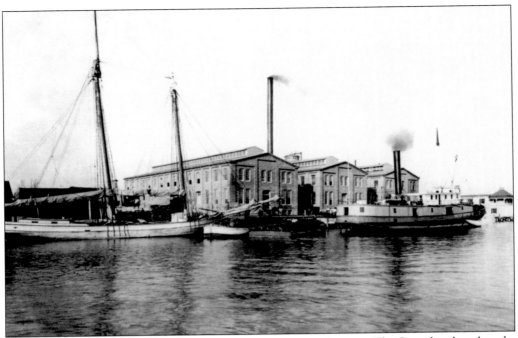

The Henry Roever Company was the producer of Blue Naptha soap. The Scott brothers bought these buildings in 1910, moving their paper business to Chester.

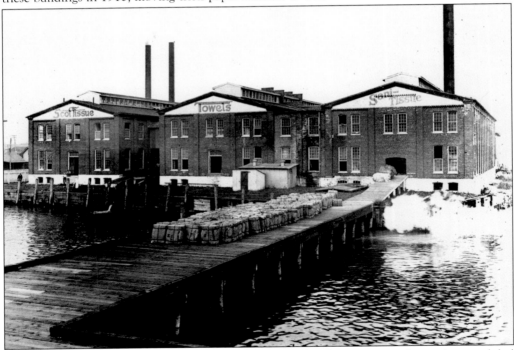

The Scott plant is shown here in 1914. It began as a local company and grew into a global corporation, merging with Kimberly Clark in 1995. The plant is still in operation today and produces over 550 tons of paper products each day. (Kimberly Clark Corporation.)

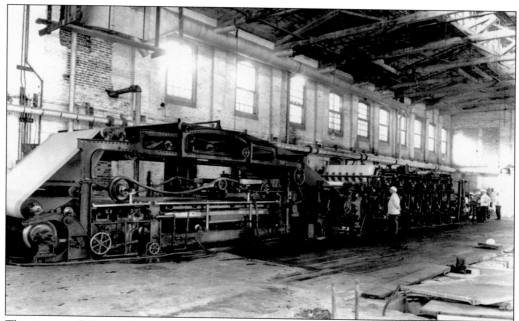

This is one of the early papermaking machines installed by Scott Paper in its Chester plant. This machine could run at speeds of up to 600 feet per minute, which led to workers in the mill being known as "the madmen of Chester." Today the mills run as fast as 5,700 feet per minute. (Kimberly Clark Corporation.)

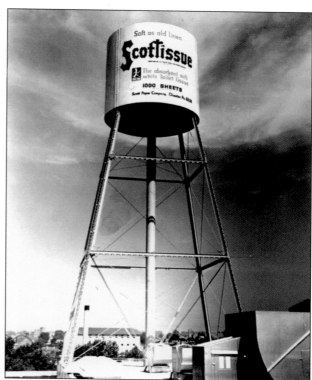

The Scott water tower was a landmark seen by residents and visitors of Chester for more than 50 years. It was removed in the early 1990s to make room for machine upgrades. (Kimberly Clark Corporation.)

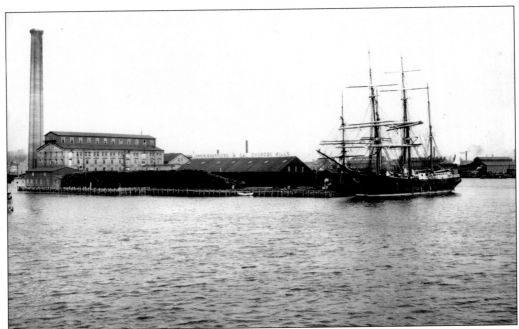

From the Delaware River, residents had a wonderful view of the Sharpless Dye-Wood Extract Company. (DCHS.)

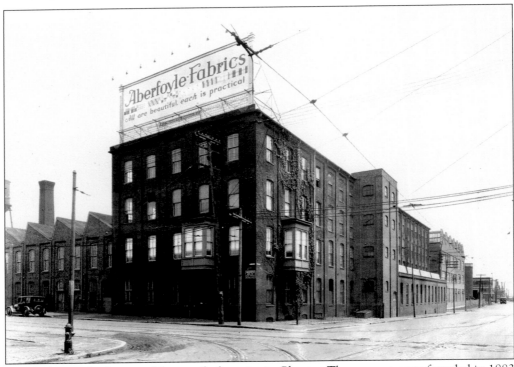

Aberfoyle was the largest of the textile factories in Chester. The company was founded in 1883 by William T. Galey.

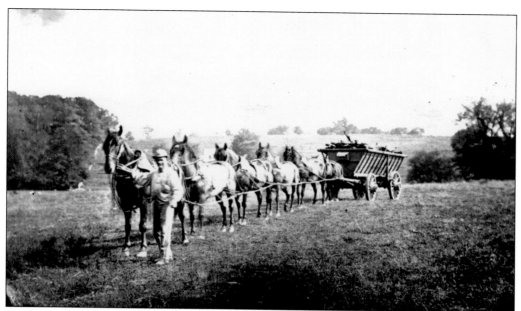

Workers are busy bringing in a load of wood and roots to be used in the making of dyes for the textile industry. Thousands of residents were employed in the yarn and fabric mills during the late 19th and the early 20th centuries before imports forced their closure. (DCHS.)

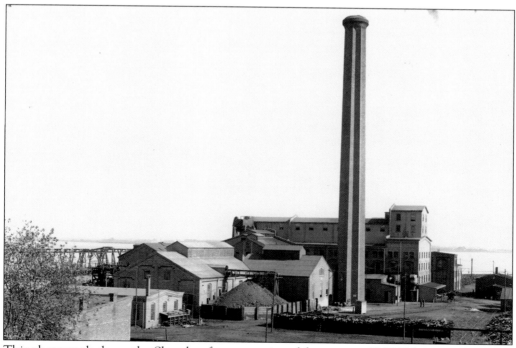

This photograph shows the Sharpless factory as viewed from town. (DCHS.)

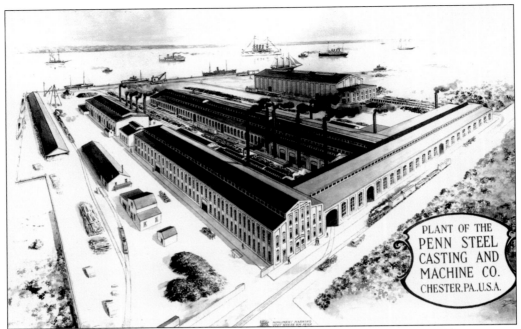

Penn Steel was one of the largest steel-casting companies in Delaware County. The company produced steel and iron products for the shipbuilding and engine works industries along the Delaware River. (DCHS.)

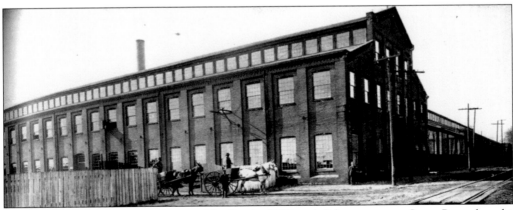

The Penn Steel factory was destroyed by fire in 1970 and did not reopen. Scott Paper bought the land and built its powerhouse there in the early 1980s. (DCHS.)

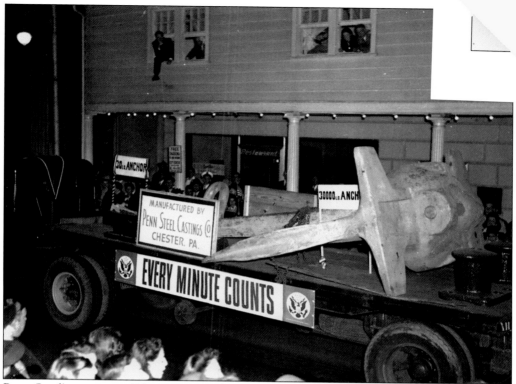

Penn Steel's motto was "No casting too large for our capacity." (DCHS.)

As a result of the shipbuilding industry in the area, there were many steelworks and ironworks located in Chester. (DCHS.)

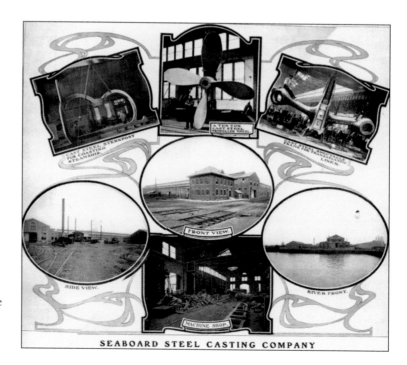

SEABOARD STEEL CASTING COMPANY

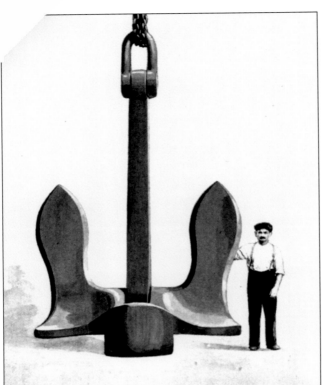

Baldt Anchor is still in business today, producing chain and anchors. (DCHS.)

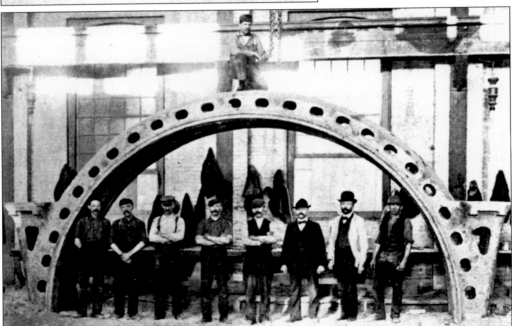

The Chester Steel Casting Company, shown here in 1903, was another of the foundries that produced products for the shipbuilding industry. The company was founded in 1870 as the McHaffie Direct Steel Castings Company and changed its name in 1873. (DCHS.)

Three

TRANSPORTATION, STORES, AND BUSINESS

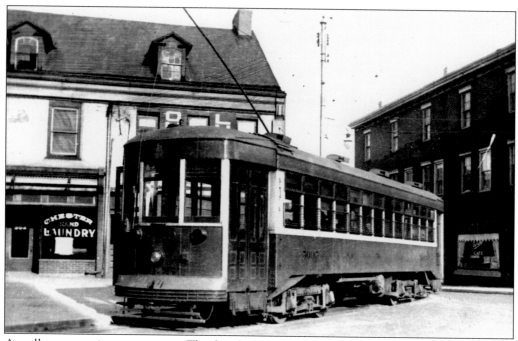

A trolley car awaits passengers at Third and Market Streets. (A. W. Maginnis.)

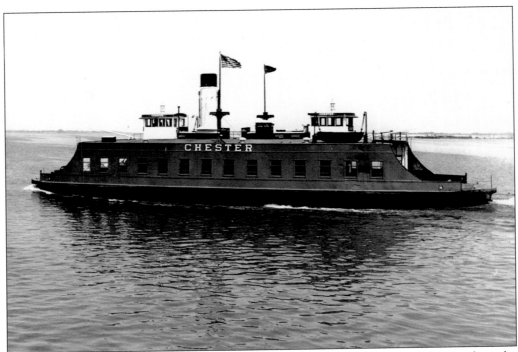

The Chester Bridgeport Ferry was started in the late 1920s and ran until 1974, when the Commodore Barry Bridge opened. (DCHS.)

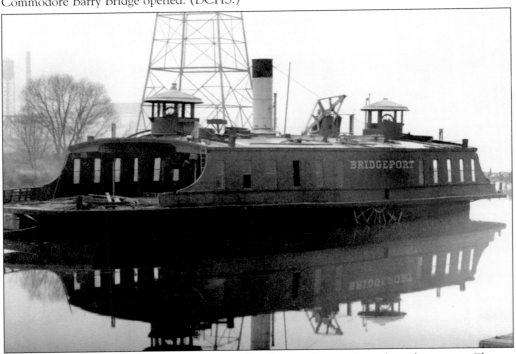

As Chester's industrial base grew, the ferry offered a way for people and goods to enter Chester from New Jersey. (DCHS.)

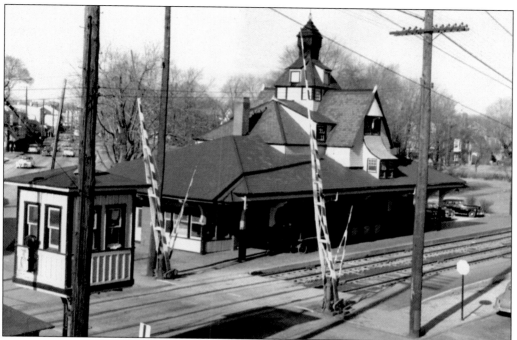

There were two railroad stations in Chester—those serving the Baltimore & Ohio and Pennsylvania Railroads. Chester lost the B&O station when Interstate 95 was built in the 1960s. (DCHS.)

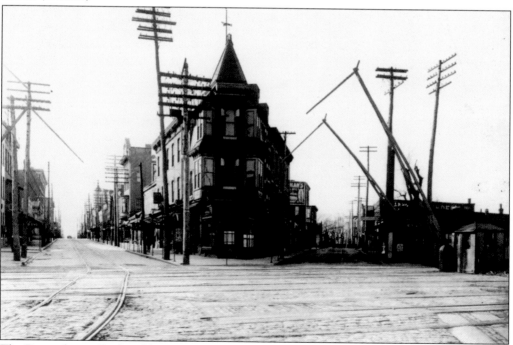

The Pennsylvania Railroad line ran through the middle of downtown at street level until it was elevated in 1903. (DCHS.)

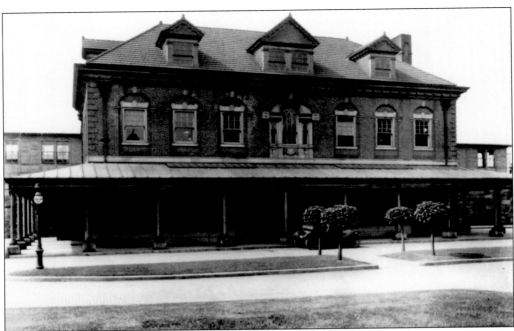

The Pennsylvania Railroad station was built 100 years ago and is still a transportation hub in Chester. (DCHS.)

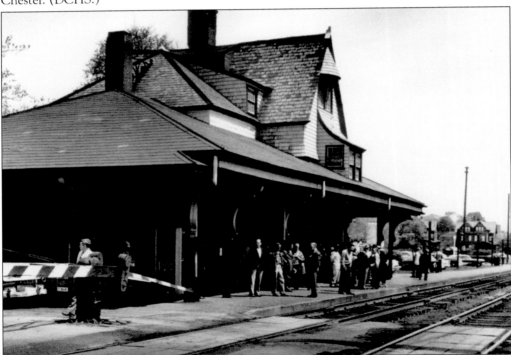

This photograph was taken on the last day that trains of the B&O stopped in Chester. The station was closed, and the tracks were relocated to make room for the building of Interstate 95 through Chester. (DCHS.)

The Chester Traction Company was just one of the companies that ran trolleys throughout the city. (A. W. Maginnis.)

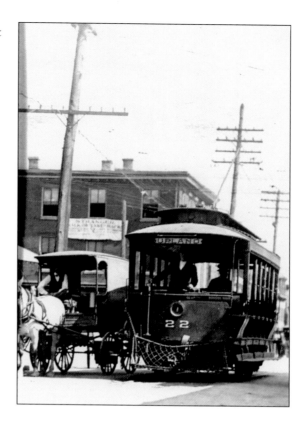

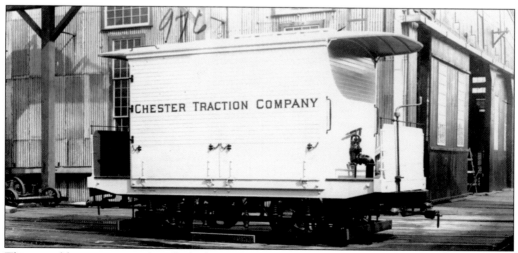

This sprinkler car was used to flush dirt and dust from the trolley tracks and to wet down the dirt streets over which they ran. (A. W. Maginnis.)

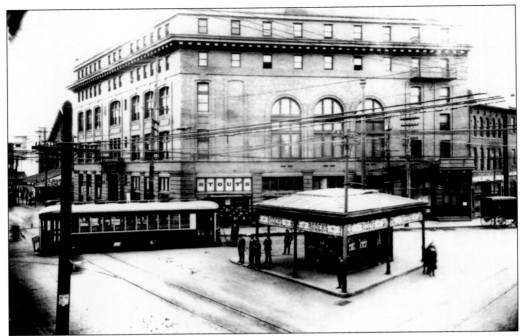

Although the trolleys are now gone and the downtown area has gone through numerous changes, the newsstand seen in this photograph still stands today. (DCHS.)

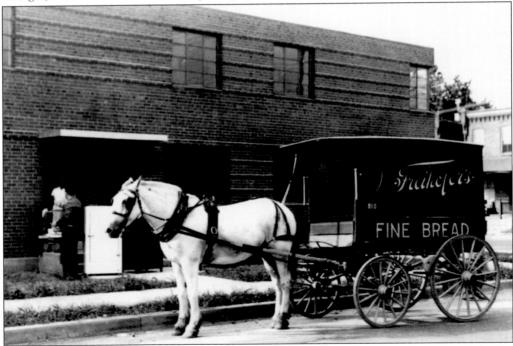

Before the days of cars and trucks, bread and milk deliveries took a great amount of time. The friendly service made up for the long delivery time, as the goods were delivered to each customer's door. (DCHS.)

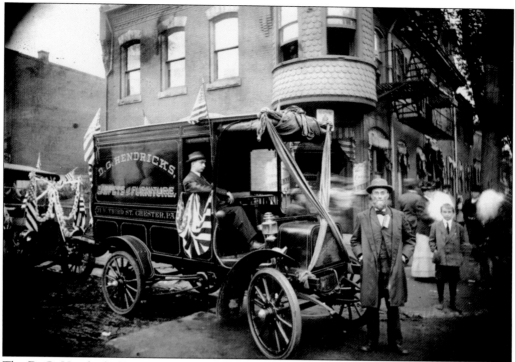

The D. G. Hendricks Furniture Company shows off its first motorized delivery truck. (DCHS.)

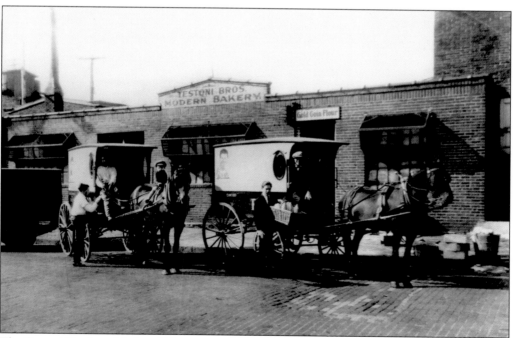

The Testoni Brothers Modern Bakery starts off another day delivering its wares. (Carmela Lewis.)

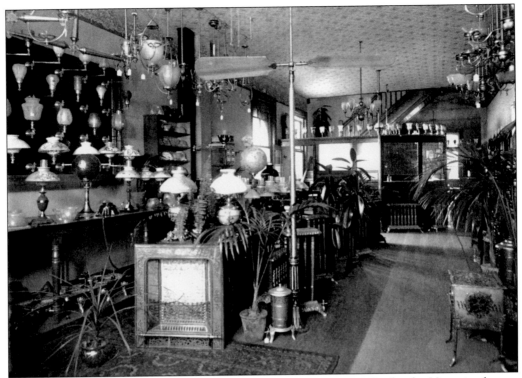

The Suburban Gas Company sold gaslights and heaters in many styles for the Victorian homes of the period. (DCHS.)

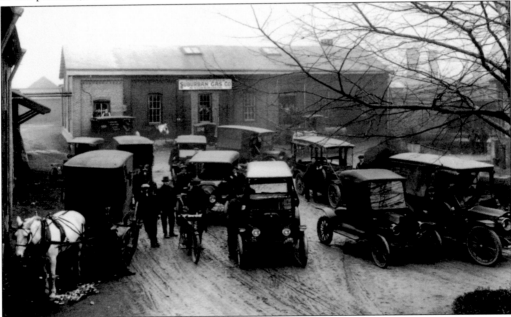

Judging by the traffic at their store, the Suburban Gas Company sold many of the goods that people needed for their horseless carriages and motorbikes. (DCHS.)

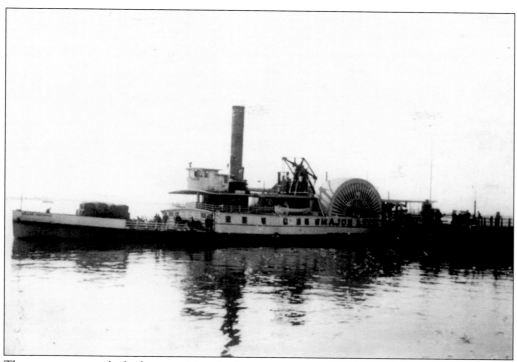

There was a great deal of competition in the river excursion industry. Pictured *c.* 1900 is the *Major Reybold*, a rear paddlewheel steamer docked in Chester. (DCHS.)

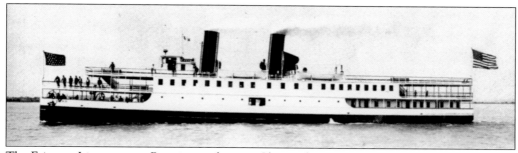

The Ericsson Line steamer *Penn* is seen leaving Chester for an excursion on the Delaware River, which was a popular way to spend a summer's day. The *Penn* was capable of speeds up to 20 knots. (DCHS.)

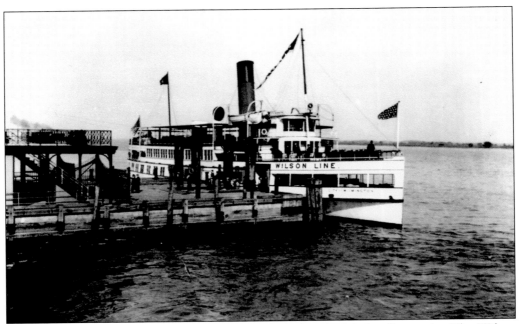

The Wilson Line steamer *City of Wilmington* is docked at the Market Street pier. The Wilson Line was one of the last excursion lines to operate out of Chester. (DCHS.)

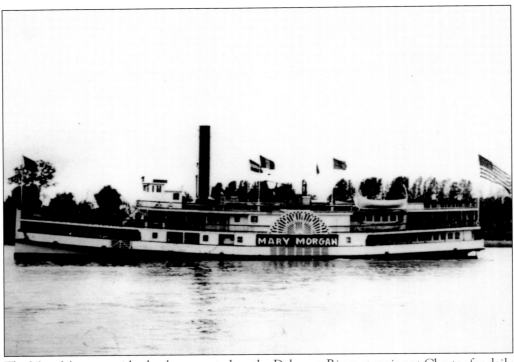

The *Mary Morgan*, a sidewheeler, operated on the Delaware River, stopping at Chester for daily excursions. (DCHS.)

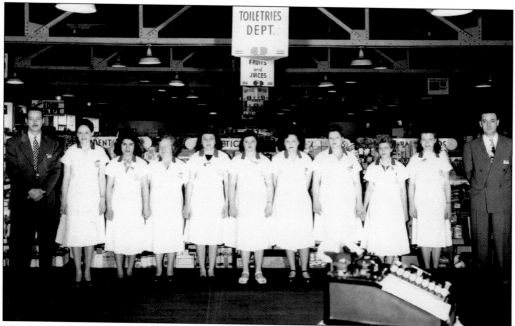

The workers of the market at Fifth and Water Streets pose in 1946. (Jean Cinabue.)

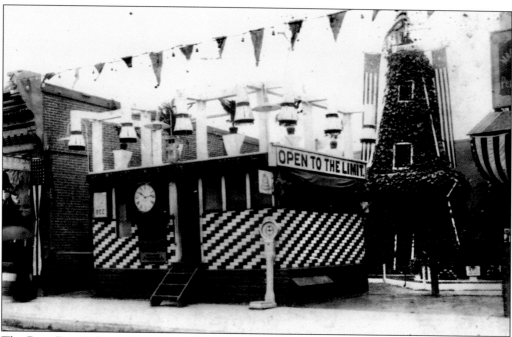

The Busy Bee Café was located on Edgemont Avenue south of Seventh Street. The café got its name from the owner, John "B" Anderson. (DCHS.)

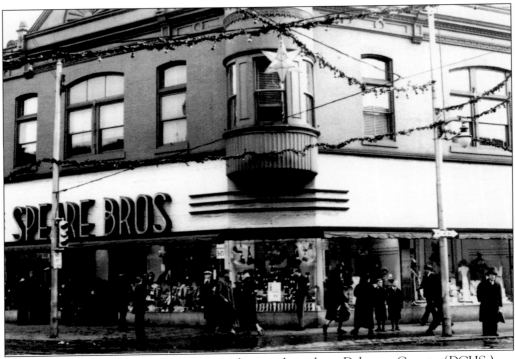

The Speare Brothers department store was known throughout Delaware County. (DCHS.)

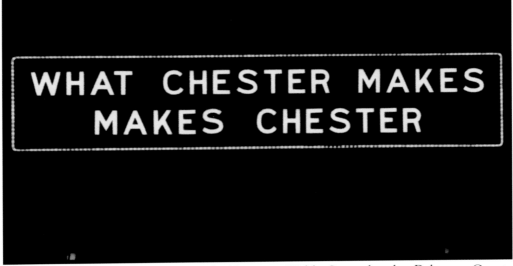

WHAT CHESTER MAKES
MAKES CHESTER

Mounted on the electric company building on Welsh Street by the Delaware County Board of Commerce, this sign reflects the prosperity Chester bustled with early in its development. (DCHS.)

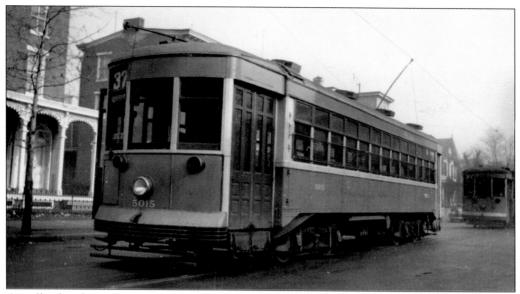

A trolley heads out for another day on the tracks in the city of Chester. (A. W. Maginnis.)

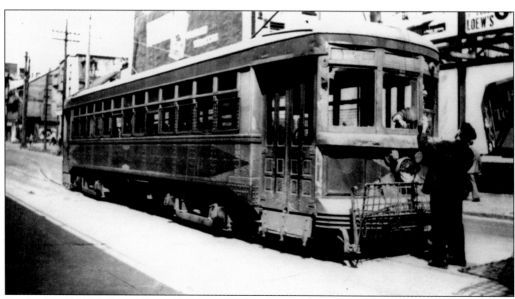

By the late 1930s, the trolley system in Chester began shutting down, a victim of the internal combustion engine. (A. W. Maginnis.)

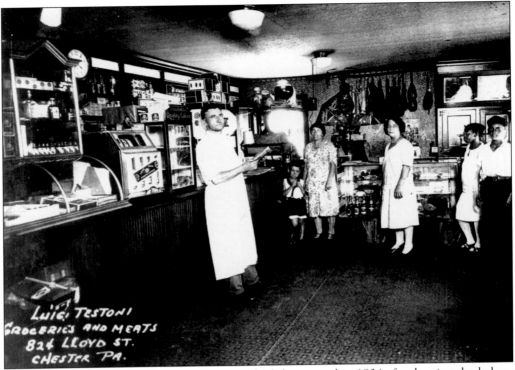

Luisi Testoni is pictured in his grocery store, which he opened in 1924 after leaving the bakery he and his brother operated. (Carmela Lewis.)

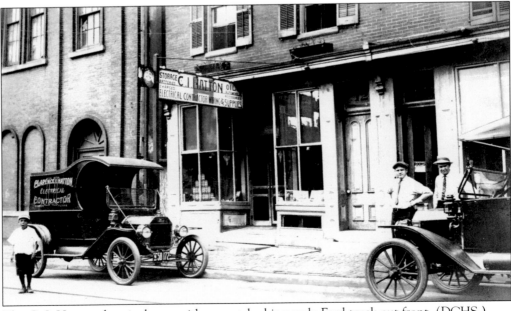

The C. I. Hatton shop is shown with a great-looking early Ford truck out front. (DCHS.)

Four

SACRED PLACES

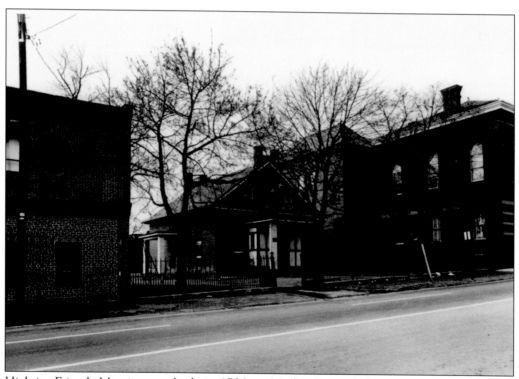

Hicksite Friends Meeting was built in 1736 on Market Street below Third Street. In 1926, they merged with the Chester Orthodox Friends Meeting, located at 24th and Chestnut Streets. (DCHS.)

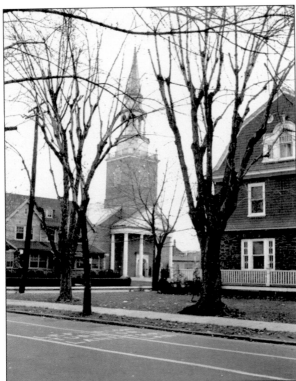

First Presbyterian Church is located at the southeast corner of Fourth and Welsh Streets. It was built in 1851. I. E. Cochran Sr. donated the land on which the church was erected. (DCHS.)

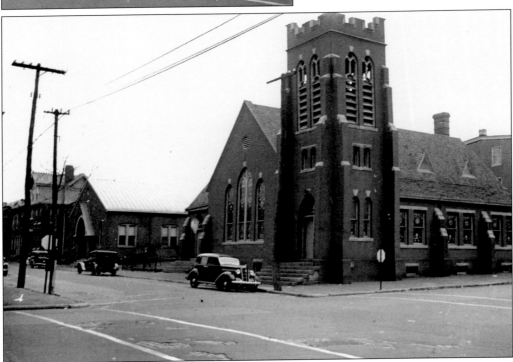

St. Michael's was started on November 1, 1874, and dedicated on November 5, 1882. (DCHS.)

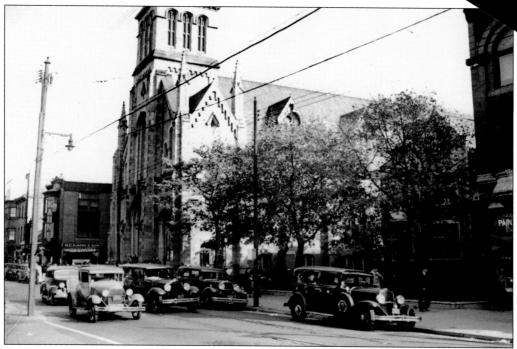

The original structure of St. Paul's was erected on January 25, 1702, on the south side of Third Street, east of Market Square. It stood until July 1850. The cornerstone of the church as it stands today was laid on November 1, 1874. (DCHS.)

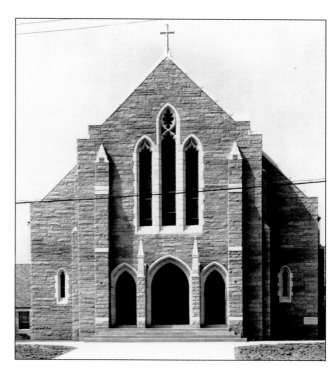

St. Robert's (now St. Katharine Drexel), located at 1920 Providence Avenue, was built on October 13, 1940. The first mass was held in the school auditorium, and this continued until the church's completion and dedication on Sunday, May 18, 1941. (St. Katherine Drexel.)

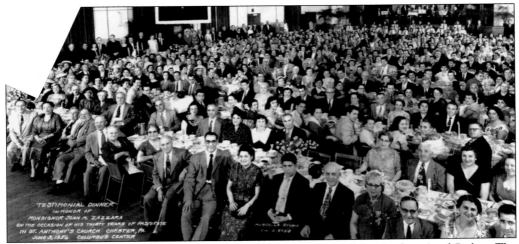

In 1912, Rev. Antonio Garritano was named the first pastor of St. Anthony's of Padua. The cornerstone of the church was laid on June 11, 1913. In September 1921, St. Anthony's School was opened. The congregation is shown at a gathering held to celebrate the event. (Al Palagruto.)

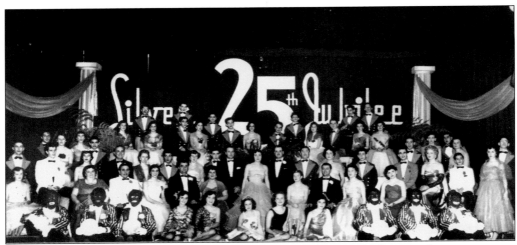

This photograph shows St. Anthony's of Padua's silver jubilee in 1938. It seems the congregation put on quite a show. (Al Palagruto.)

Madison Street Methodist Episcopal Church is shown here. In 1818, John Kelley held services in his own home and subsequently services were held in the Colonial Court House for many years. In 1830, a stone church was erected on Second Street at the corner of Bevans Court. (DCHS.)

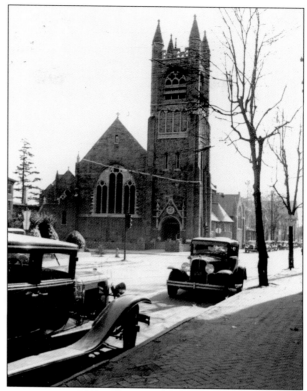

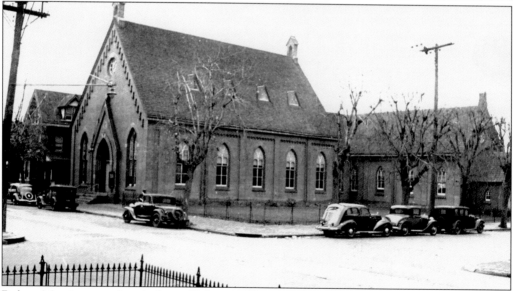

Robert Morris was a slave in lower Delaware. He was a favorite of his bankrupt master and was sold to Charles Lloyd of the Blue Bell Tavern in Kingsessing for $300 on the condition that when he attained the age of 30 he was to be freed. After being freed, Robert came to Chester and organized the Union African Methodist Episcopal Church. In 1831, a frame structure was raised on Welsh Street, which was replaced in the 1880s by a stone structure. (DCHS.)

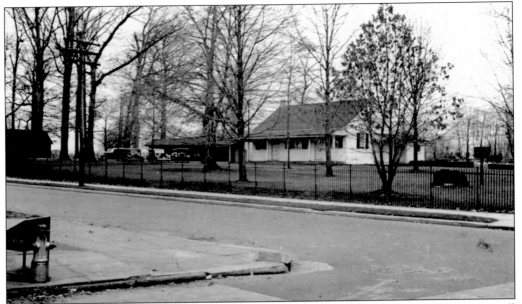

The Friends meetinghouse at 24th and Chestnut Streets was built in 1829. It is still open. (DCHS.)

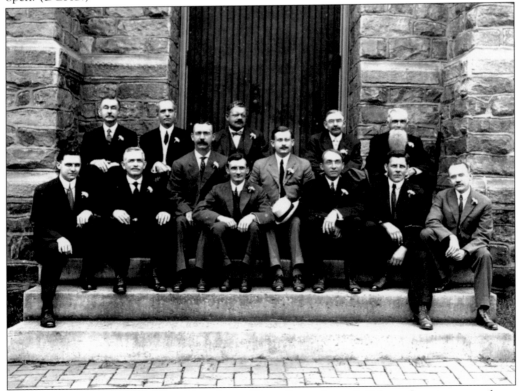

Members of the First Baptist Church, at West Seventh and Fulton Streets, pose for a photograph. (DCHS.)

St. Nicholas Russian Church served the Russian community in Chester. There were many ethnic groups that made Chester home and built churches and centers, like this one, in which to meet. (DCHS.)

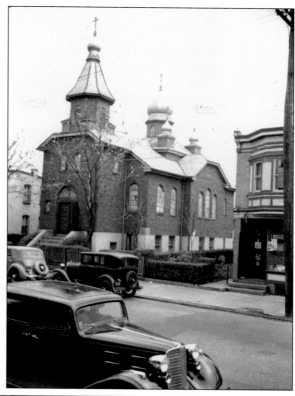

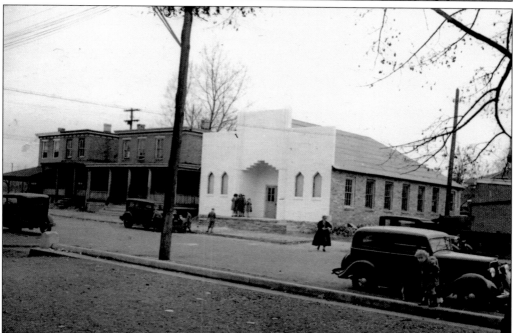

The Gospel Tabernacle Church, pictured here in the late 1930s, is another piece of Chester's rich and diverse religious heritage. (DCHS.)

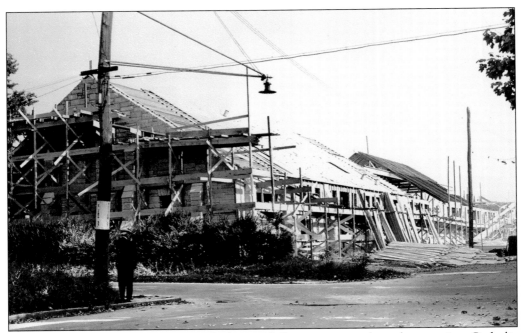

The new St. Robert's School was built in 1940 to accommodate the growing Catholic population in Chester. (St. Katherine Drexel.)

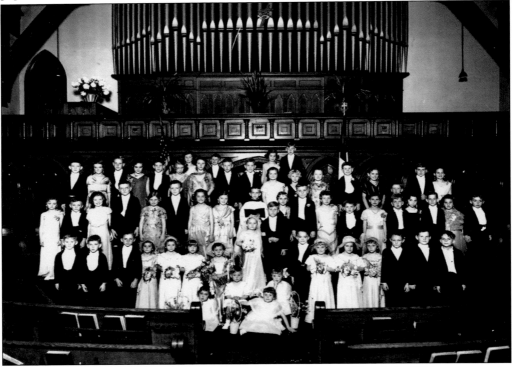

Tom Thumb weddings, such as this one held at the First Baptist Church in 1934, were popular events to photograph and attend.

Five

PEOPLE

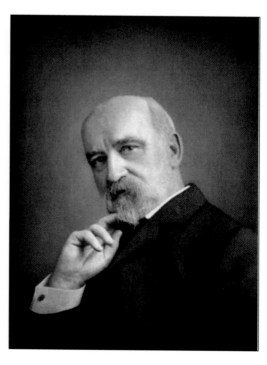

Henry Graham Ashmead, Delaware County
historian, wrote several books on Chester
more than 100 years ago. (DCHS.)

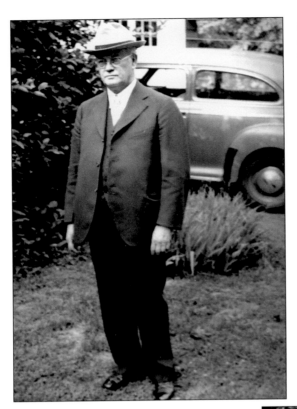

Chester Forrest Baker was an engineer and surveyor. He had offices in the Crozer building. He was an avid photographer of the area's historical past. (DCHS.)

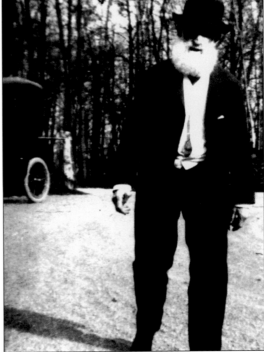

Alfred O. Deshong, a prominent resident of Chester, was a financier, industrialist, and philanthropist. In 1913, he left his estate to the people of Chester with plans for a museum to be built to house his extensive collection of rare art. (DCHS.)

Samuel A. Crozer was an Upland resident. He was director of the Delaware County National Bank and an active member of Delaware County Historical Society, founded in 1895. (DCHS.)

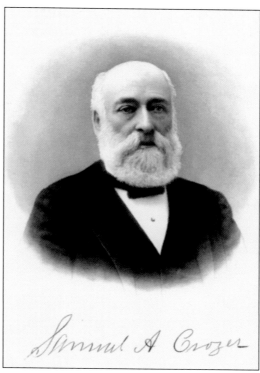

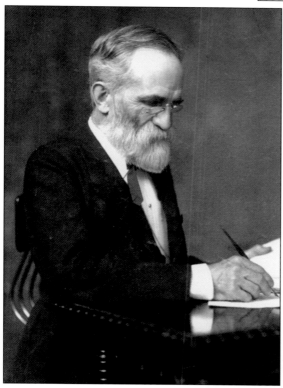

John B. Hinkson was educated at Oak Grove School, Grays Academy, and Lafayette College. He studied as an attorney in the office of John M. Broomall. In 1893, he was elected as the mayor of Chester. (DCHS.)

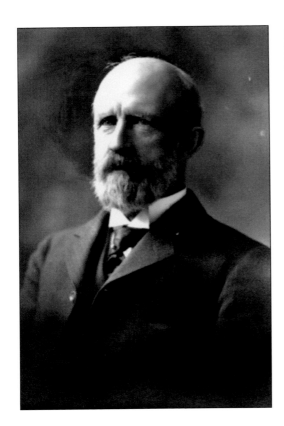

Frank Black was a prominent businessman. He served as president of Chester National Bank. (DCHS.)

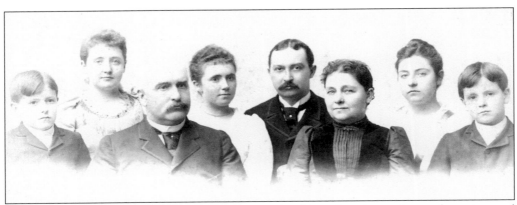

John B. Roach poses with his family. Roach owned a shipyard and manufactured monitor and ironside ships for the navy. (DCHS.)

William Provost Jr. was a leading contractor and builder whose work included residences and large manufacturing plants. Some of his projects were Penn Steel Casting, the Chester High School, Aberfoyle Manufacturing, St. Paul's, and Third Presbyterian Church. (DCHS.)

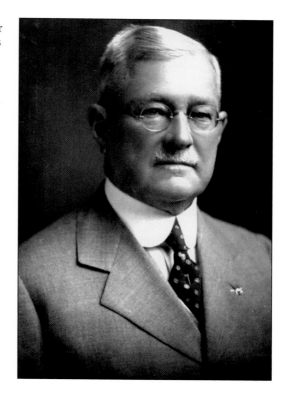

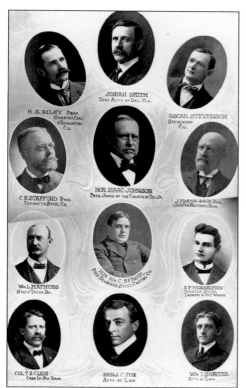

This page from the 1903 Chester book by Ashmead depicts important businessmen from the city. The book was handed out by the businesses he included in the book. The historical society has seen several with different company's names on the cover. (DCHS.)

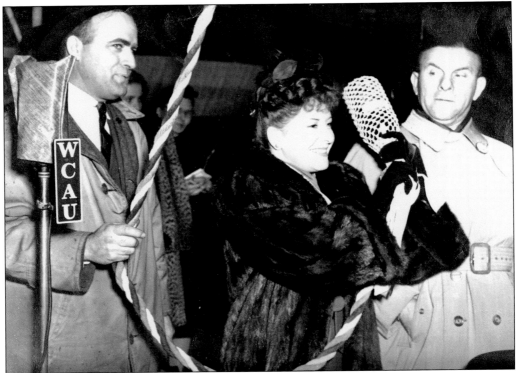

George Burns (right) and Gracie Allen prepare to christen the *Hubbardton* at its launch in 1944. (DCHS.)

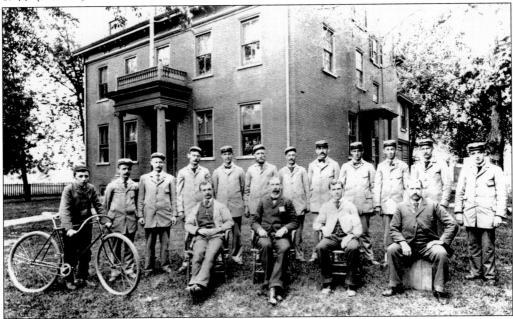

This photograph of postal delivery boys from the turn of the century looks back at the days of the telegraph. (DCHS.)

Two Crozer Seminary students enjoy a summer's day in Chester Park in the early part of the 20th century.

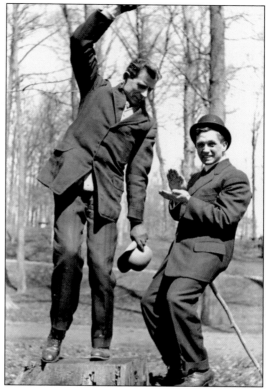

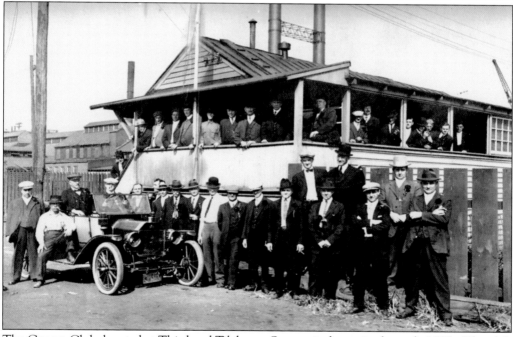

The George Club, located at Third and Tilghman Streets, is shown in the early 1900s. The club had one rule: your name had to be George in order to become a member. (Dorothy Smith.)

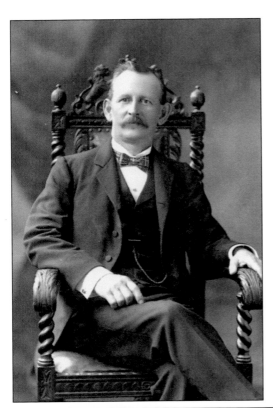

William J. McClure, a longtime Republican political boss, poses for a photograph taken by Chester F. Baker. (DCHS.)

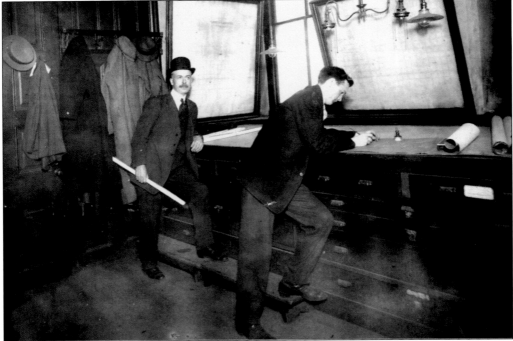

Chester F. Baker is seen at work as an assistant engineer for the city of Chester. (DCHS.)

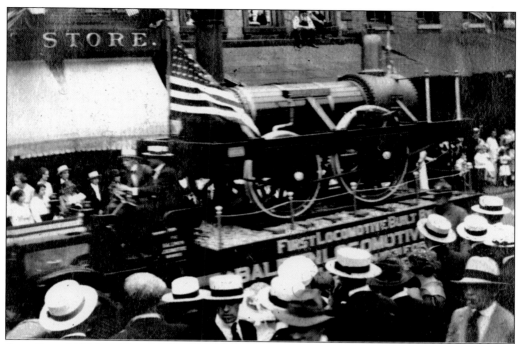

A replica of *Old Ironsides*, the first Baldwin locomotive, is on its way to be displayed in front of the Colonial Court House in 1948.

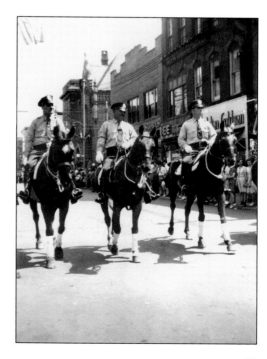

Policemen on horseback parade down Market Street in the early 1950s. (Smedley.)

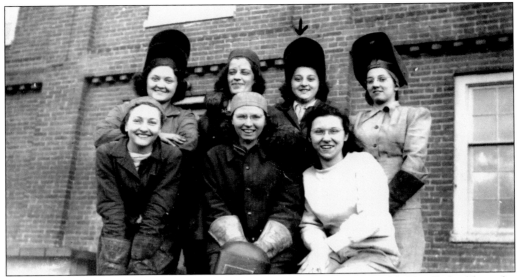

Women welders work at the Sun Shipbuilding Company during World War II, building the Liberty ships that made the company famous. (Jean Cinabue.)

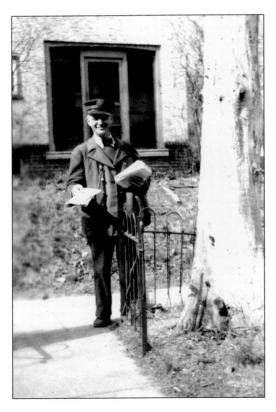

Postman Bob Watts makes deliveries in Chester. It is thought that he knew all of the people on his route. (Marje McNiff.)

Six

EDUCATION IN CHESTER

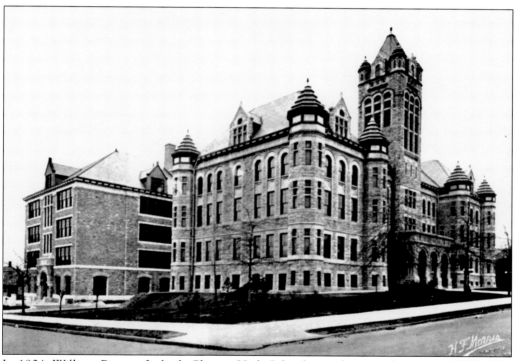

In 1904, William Provost Jr. built Chester High School out of granite for a cost of $168,000. Chester High consisted of 44 rooms and castlelike towers and was located at Ninth and Fulton Streets. Most residents in Chester attended Chester High. The first class of the new school graduated in 1905 with T. S. Cole as the first principal. Students attended the school until 1968, when it was gutted and razed due to a fire. Chester High School was one of the landmarks of the city and a top selling postcard view for visitors to the city. Everyone will remember Chester High in the school ring's black onyx stone. (DCHS.)

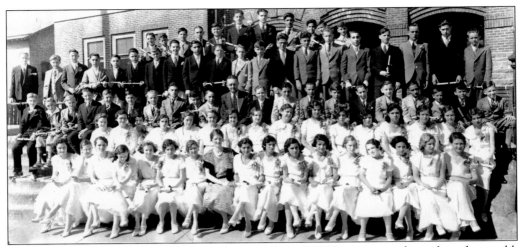

The members of Franklin School's graduating class of 1929 appear ready to face the world. (Carmela Lewis.)

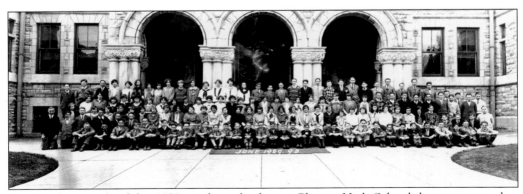

As this photograph of the 1929 ninth-grade class at Chester High School demonstrates, class size was not always an issue. (DCHS.)

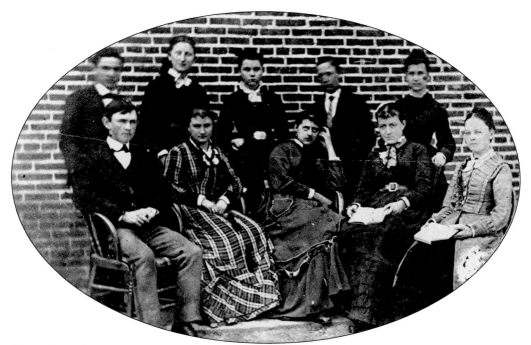

Pictured is Chester High School's graduating class of 1875. This was the first graduating class at the school, which was also known as the Starr School. (DCHS.)

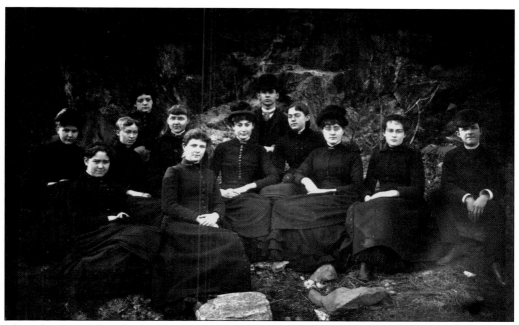

The Chester High School graduating class of 1885 poses for this unusual class picture in the park. (DCHS.)

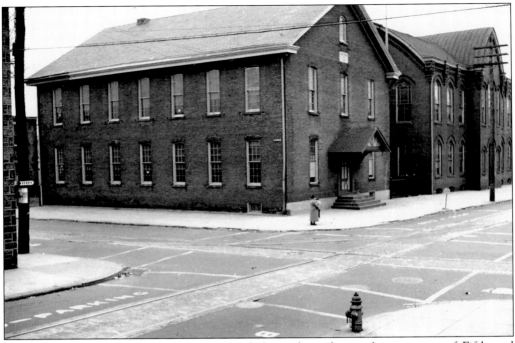

The school in front was the Harvey School, located on the southeast corner of Fifth and Welsh Streets. To the right is the Starr School, which was the original name for Chester High School. (DCHS.)

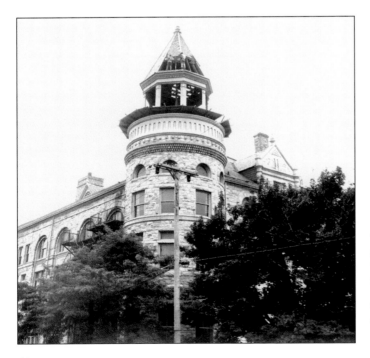

The John Larkin Jr. Grammar School was located at Ninth and Crosby Streets and was built in 1894 by Joel Lane. He also built the original *Chester Times* building, which closed in 1975. (DCHS.)

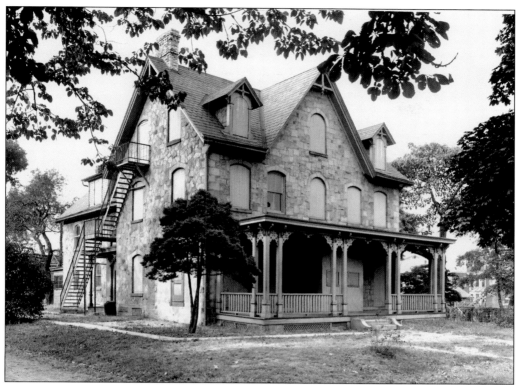

Shown here is the Eyre School Annex, which was a part of Chester High School. It was also the former residence of Gen. William G. Price Jr. and his wife. (DCHS.)

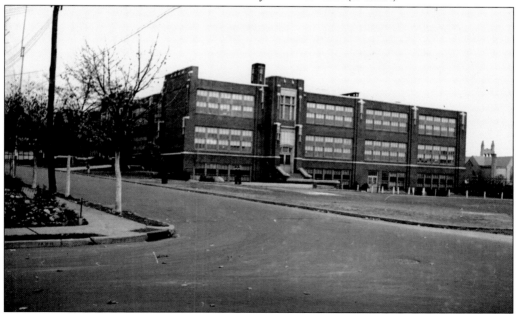

Smedley Junior High School was located at 17th and Upland Streets. The school was opened in 1924 and still operates as a middle school. The first principal was Margret Stetser. (DCHS.)

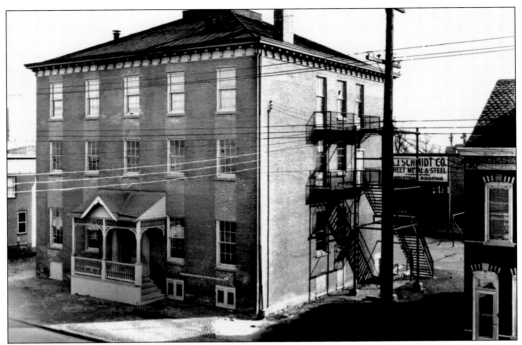

The Gartside Elementary School was located at west Second and Franklin Streets. It closed in 1958. (DCHS.)

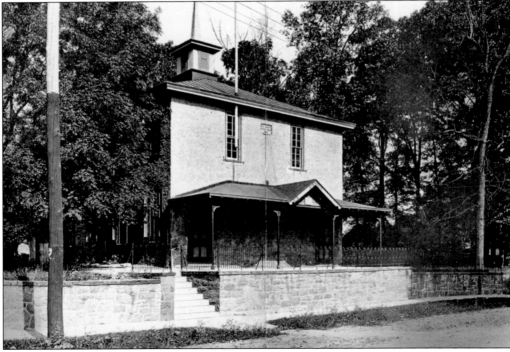

The Oak Grove School was located on 24th Street west of Chestnut Street. The original building was erected in 1813, and it became the John Wetherill School in 1905. (DCHS.)

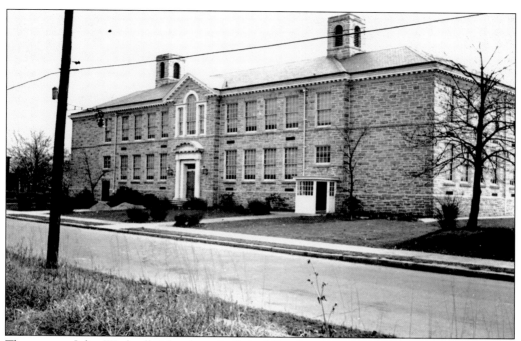

The present John Wetherll School was built in 1931. It is located on 24th Street just south of Upland Street. (DCHS.)

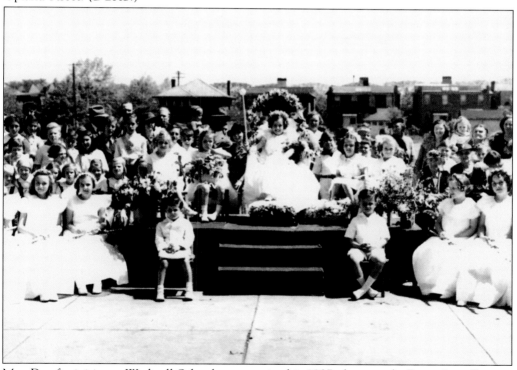

May Day festivities at Wetherll School are seen in this 1937 photograph. Betty Ann Gaynor, the queen of May Day, is in the center of the photograph. (DCHS.)

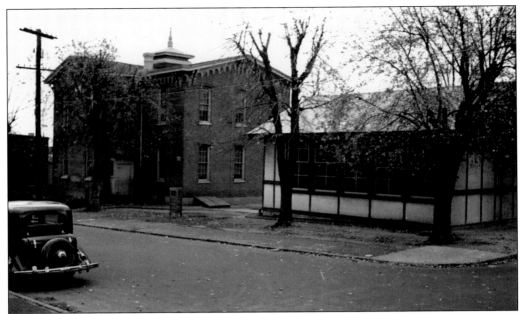

George Jones was the first African American teacher to teach African American students in Chester. In 1853, he opened and operated a school in the basement of Asbury African Methodist Episcopal Church on Second Street above Market Street. The George Jones School, built in 1902, was named in his honor. It was located at 17th and Walnut Streets. (DCHS.)

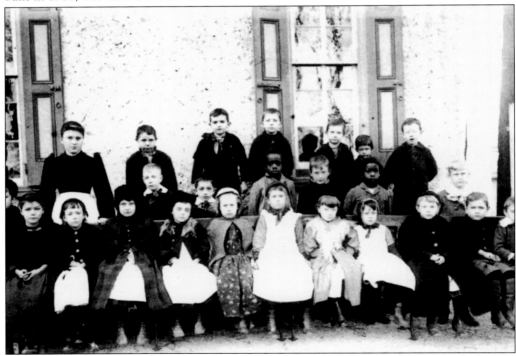

This photograph of an early grammar school class at the Oak Grove School dates back to 1890. The teacher is in the back left of photograph. (DCHS.)

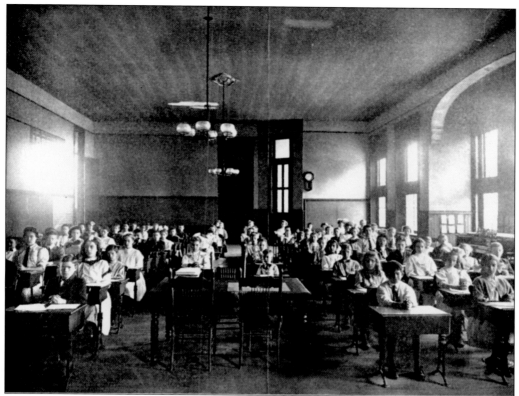

The assembly room of the Starr School, which was named after Dr. Samuel Starr, is seen in the early 1900s. This school, like many others, had large classrooms that could hold 80 students. (DCHS.)

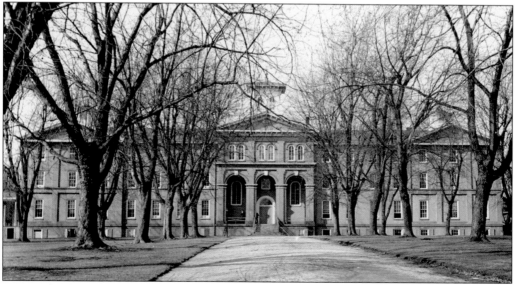

Crozer Theological Seminary was established by the Crozer family in memory of their father, John P. Crozer. He passed away on March 11, 1866, after many years of serving the community.

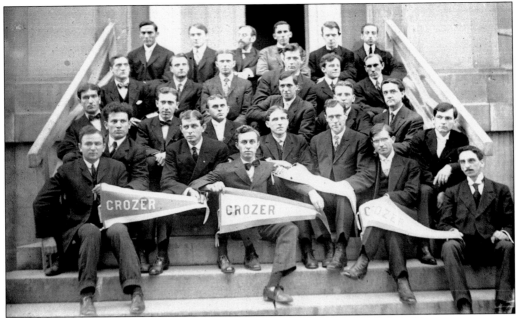

Crozer Theological Seminary students from the early 1900s pose in front of the seminary.

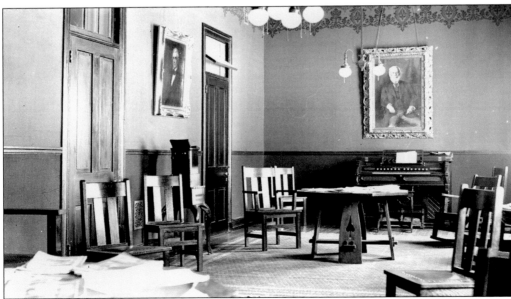

The interior of the Crozer Theological Seminary is shown in this photograph. The school was a Baptist theological seminary.

A Crozer Theological Seminary student poses in the park for a friend between his studies at the seminary.

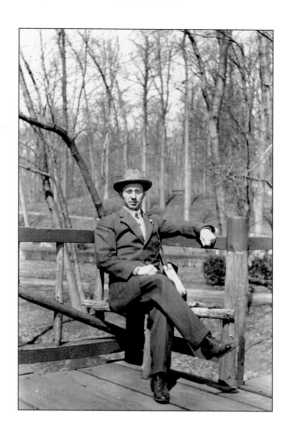

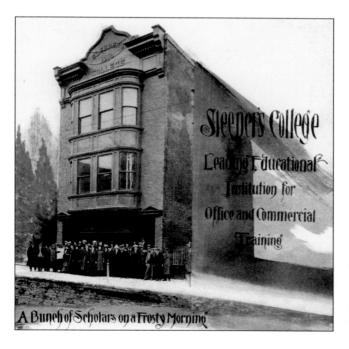

A Bunch of Scholars on a Frosty Morning

Sleepers Business College was located at 625 Welsh Street. This college taught secretarial skills and accounting to young men and women who may not have attended or graduated high school. (Smith, 1914.)

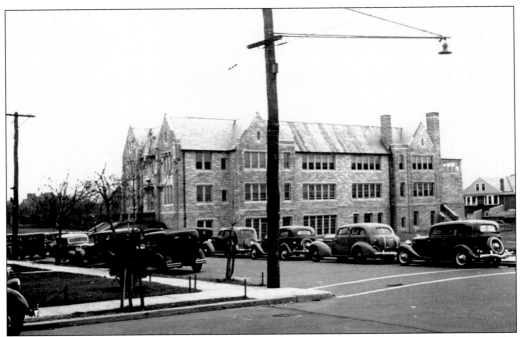

The first St. James High School, seen here, was originally the St. Robert's School before the new church and school were built. The building still stands behind the current site. (DCHS.)

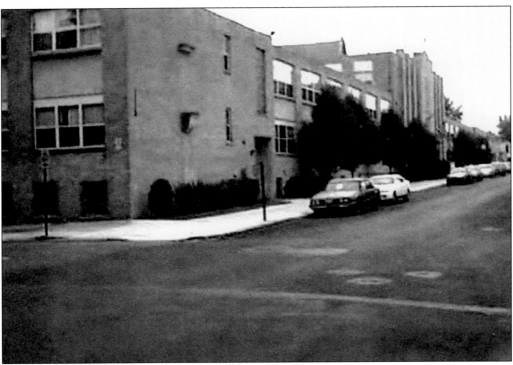

During the 1950s, many additions were made to St. James High School.

This is a page from the 1903 Ashmead book *Souvenir History of Chester*, which shows the Lincoln and Larkin Schools.

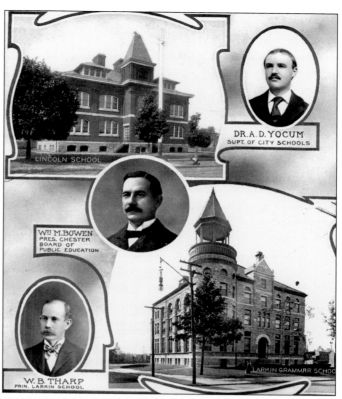

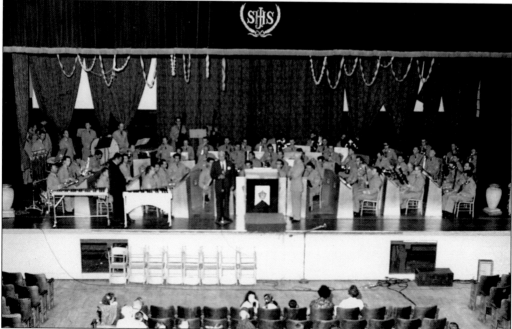

Pictured is a Smedley Junior High School assembly featuring the U.S. Army band in concert in 1958.

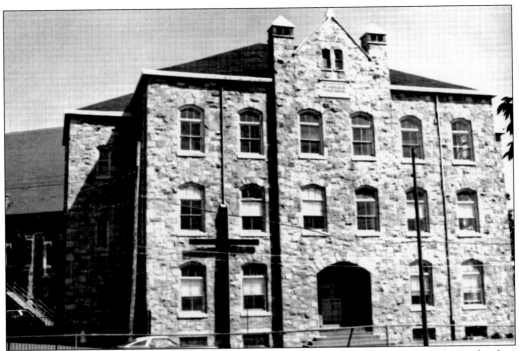

The St. Michael's school was located at Seventh Street. It was built in 1871 and was the first parish school in Delaware County. (DCHS.)

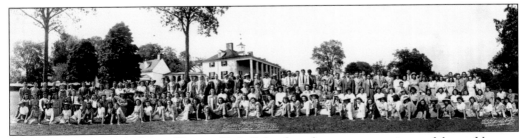

This 1941 photograph shows Chester High School students on an outing to Mount Vernon. These seniors seem to be enjoying the trip.

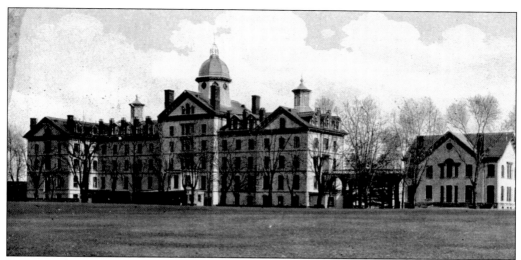

In September 1868, the Pennsylvania Military Academy moved into its newly completed building, Old Main, located to the northeast portion of the city. It was a landmark, presenting a prominent appearance when viewed from the north or east approaching Chester, and especially from the Delaware River. Col. Theodore Hyatt, the academy's founder, served as the president from 1853 to 1887.

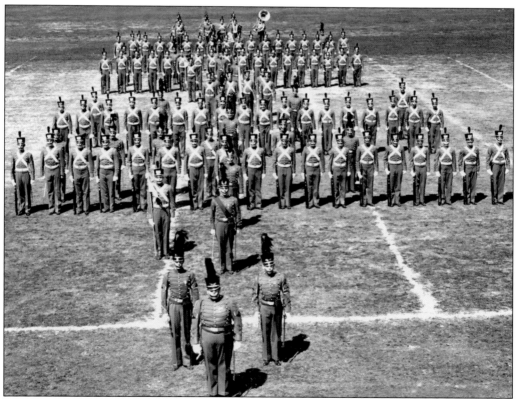

The Pennsylvania Military College color guard is seen in 1937 on the parade grounds. (Widener Archives.)

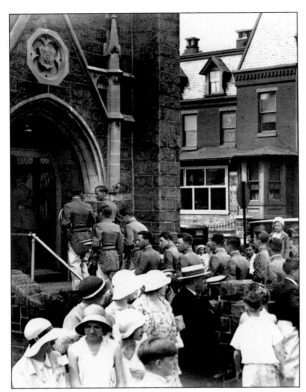

Pennsylvania Military College cadets enter the St. Paul's Episcopal Church, at Ninth and Madison Streets, for Sunday services. Cadets in uniform were a common sight in Chester during days when Widener University was Pennsylvania Military College. (Widener Archives.)

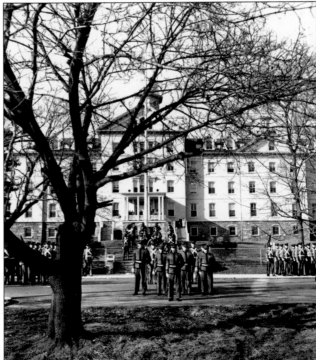

Cadets stand in formation in front of Old Main at Pennsylvania Military College. This is another common sight to visitors driving by the school. (Widener Archives.)

Col. Charles Hyatt was the second person in his family to run the school. (DCHS.)

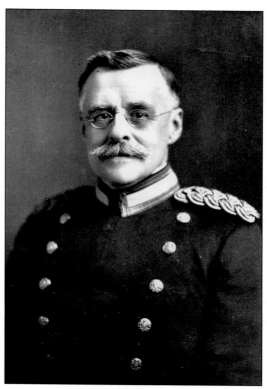

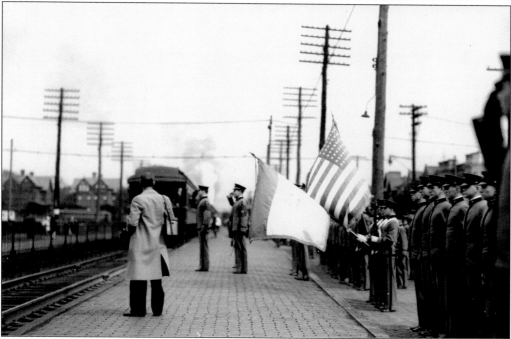

Pennsylvania Military College cadets perform the 10-second salute for Pres. Herbert Hoover as he travels through Chester by train. (Widener Archives.)

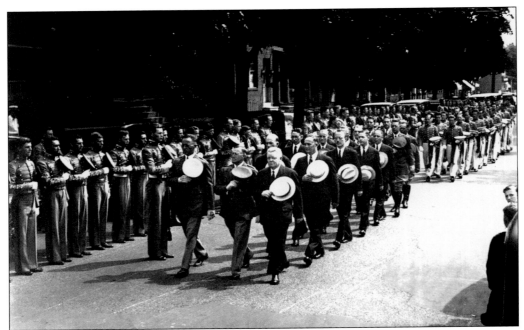

John Wanamaker, General Pershing, and Colonel Hyatt are seen on campus at Pennsylvania Military College on June 15, 1921. (Widener Archives.)

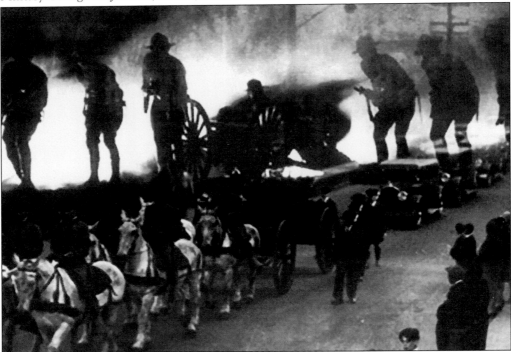

Seen is an accidental double exposure of cadets superimposed on Col. Charles Hyatt's funeral procession. Charles Hyatt served as president of Pennsylvania Military College from 1888 to 1930. (Widener Archives.)

Seven

SPORTS AND ACTIVITIES

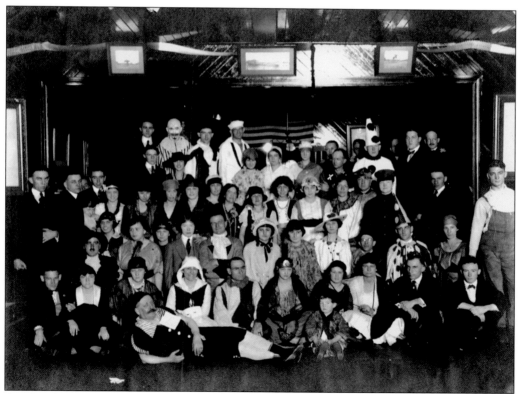

On October 25, 1919, employees and friends of the Delaware County Trust Company enjoy a night of music and activities at the Alpha Boat Club. (DCHS.)

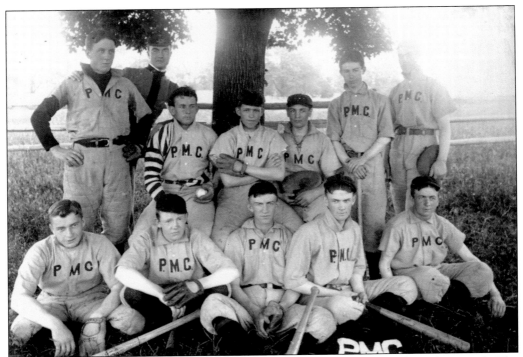

Members of 1897 Pennsylvania Military College varsity baseball team pose for a photograph. The team consisted of only 11 members, which is small by today's standard. (Widener Archives.)

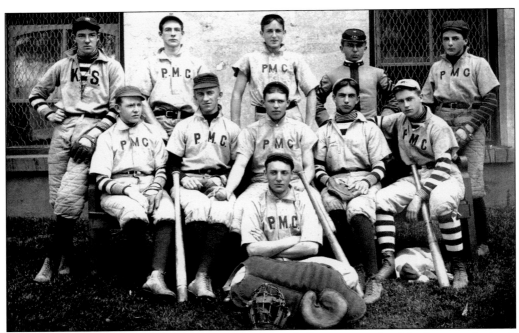

The 1899 Pennsylvania Military College varsity baseball team pose for this photograph. Look at how small the glove is on the hand of the person on the right. (Widener Archives.)

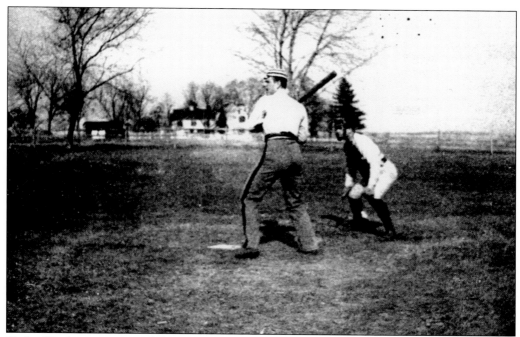

Cadet Weeks, a member of the 1900 Pennsylvania Military College cadet baseball team, steps up to bat. (Widener Archives.)

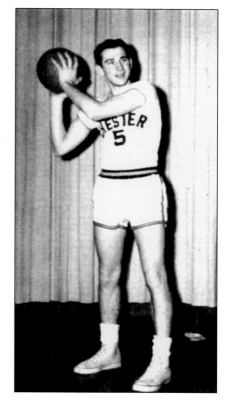

Captain Lazek of the 1955 Chester High basketball team set the standard for Chester High basketball for the next 50 years. (CHS yearbook.)

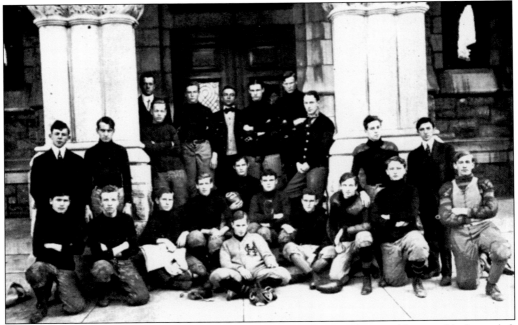

The 1907 Chester High School football team poses in full gear. Their padding and helmets left much to be desired compared to the equipment used today. (DCHS.)

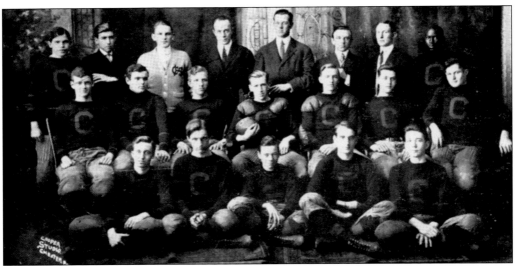

The 1918 Chester High School football team was a great-looking group of boys who were always ready to take the field. (DCHS.)

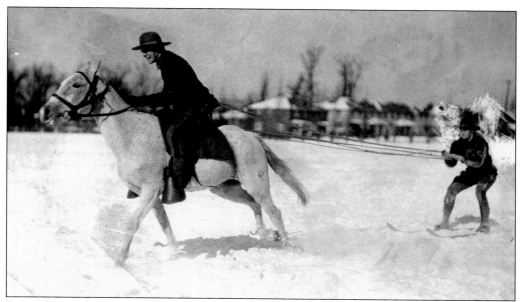

Pennsylvania Military College cadets try their hand at horse-skiing in the early 1900s. (Widener Archives.)

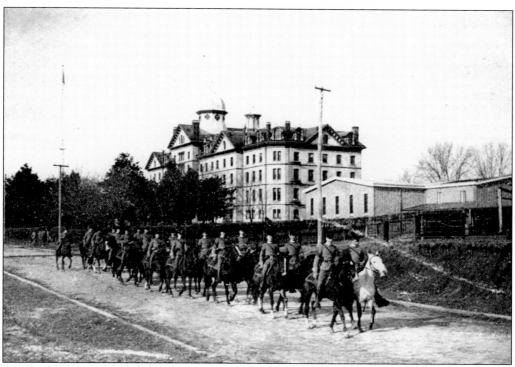

The Pennsylvania Military College Calvary Corps are pictured in 1894 on the parade grounds in front of Old Main. This is a sight many have never seen today. (Widener Archives.)

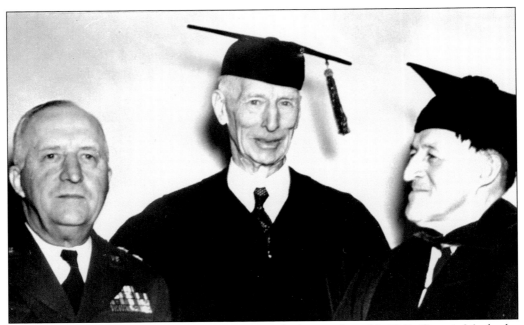

Pennsylvania Military College commencement took place on June 10, 1941. Connie Mack, the owner of the Philadelphia Athletics, receives an honorary degree. Pictured, from left to right, are Lt. Gen. H. Drum, Connie Mack, and Frank Hyatt. (Widener Archives.)

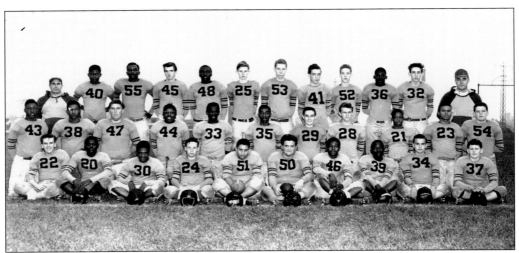

Chester High football coach James Vermeychuk poses with his team in 1954. (CHS yearbook.)

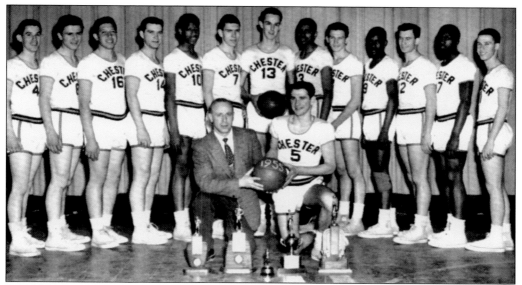

In 1955, the Chester High basketball team was a runner up in the state championship. With 26 consecutive wins, this team had the longest winning streak in the school's history. (CHS yearbook.)

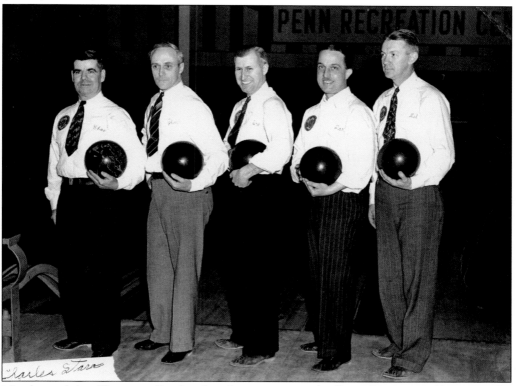

Members of the Chester police bowling league pose at the Penn Recreation Center in the 1940s. Charles Starr is on the far left. The others are, from left to right, Jim, Irv, Marty, and Mel. (Eleanor Starr.)

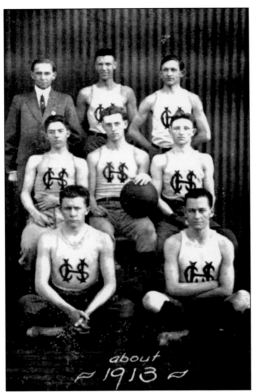

Coach Boell poses with the 1913 Chester High School basketball team. The athletes are dressed in early sports attire. (DCHS.)

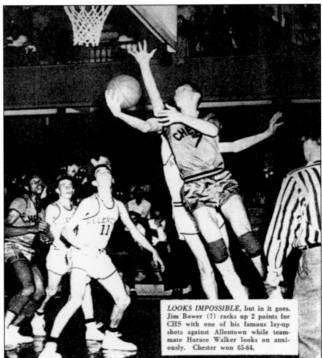

LOOKS IMPOSSIBLE, but in it goes. Jim Bower (7) racks up 2 points for CHS with one of his famous lay-up shots against Allentown while teammate Horace Walker looks on anxiously. Chester won 65-64.

Jim Bower racks up two points for Chester High with his famous lay-up against Allentown. (CHS yearbook.)

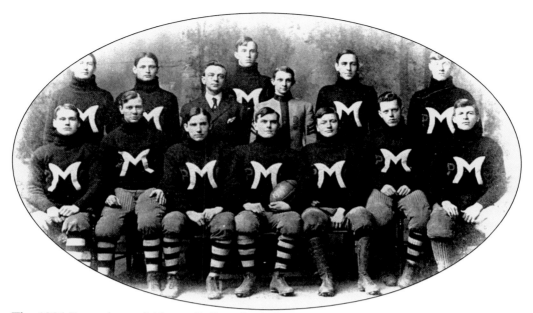

The 1906 Pennsylvania Military College football team is shown here. In those days, athletes played both sides of the ball, offence and defense. (Widener Archives.)

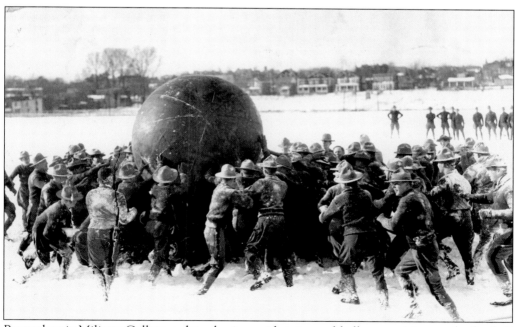

Pennsylvania Military College cadets play in a midwinter pushball competition on the football field in the 1920s. (Widener Archives.)

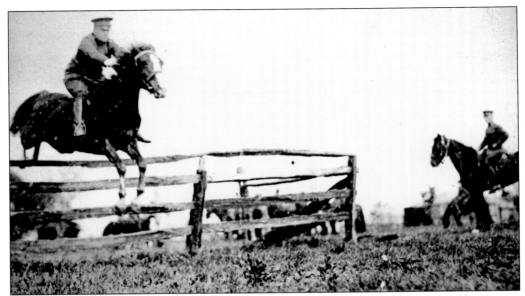

The Pennsylvania Military College steeplechase is seen in the 1900s. Back then, Chester was not far from open fields. (Widener Archives.)

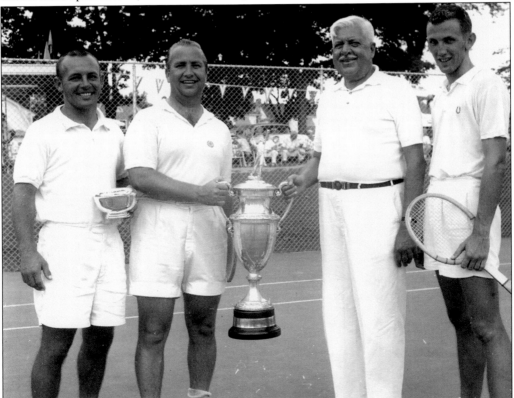

In this view, Clarence Smedley receives the winner's cup for victory in the Chester Park tennis tournament. (Smedley.)

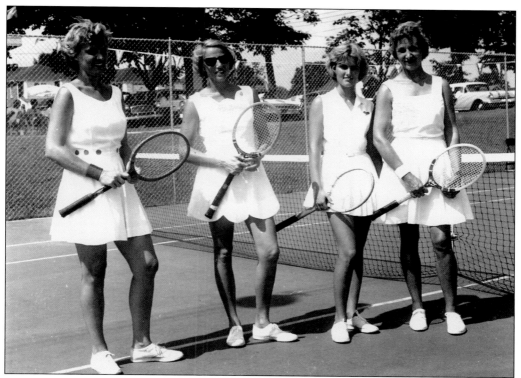

Tennis players pose at Chester Park in the 1950s. The park was a great place for summertime fun. (Smedley.)

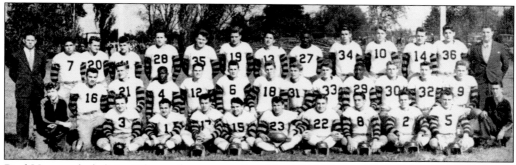

Paul Vermeychuk (No. 22) was the co-captain of the 1946 Chester High School football team. (CHS yearbook.)

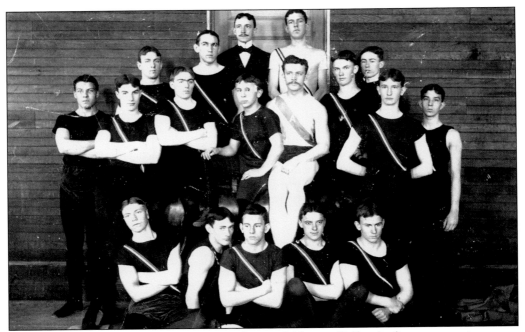

The 1896 gymnastics team was Pennsylvania Military College's first gymnastics team. (Widener Archives.)

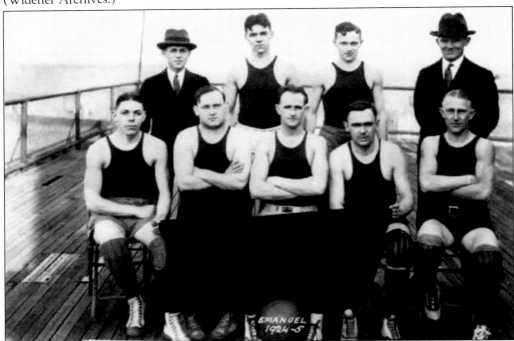

Members of the 1924–1925 Emmanuel Baptist Church champion basketball team pose for this photograph. Members are, from left to right, as follows: (first row) Bill Crystle Jr., Midge Kimber, Jesse Francis, Bill Hill, and Ed Hollwood; (second row) Rev. Eric Ostrerle, George Ackerman, Gilbert Martin, and Tom Brown. (Oldchesterpa.com.)

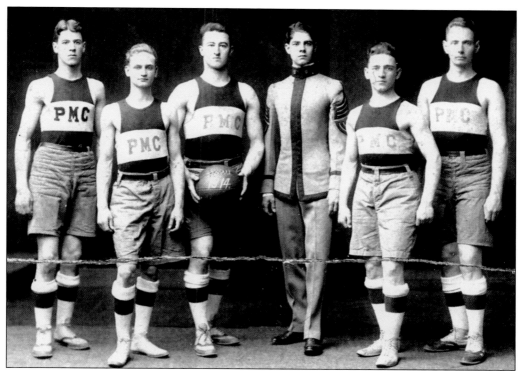

Judging by the look of determination on their faces, the 1914 Pennsylvania Military College varsity basketball team is ready to take the court. (Widener Archives.)

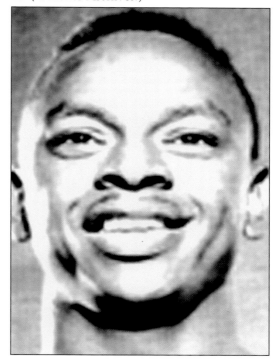

Horace Walker played for Chester High School from 1953 to 1957. He was a two-time All-American for the Clippers and a third-team All-American for Michigan State University. He played one season for the Chicago Zephyrs. (CHS yearbook.)

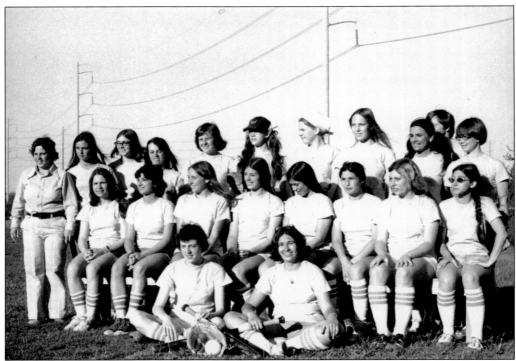

The 1974 Pennsylvania Military College girls' varsity softball team poses for a photograph. (Widener Archives.)

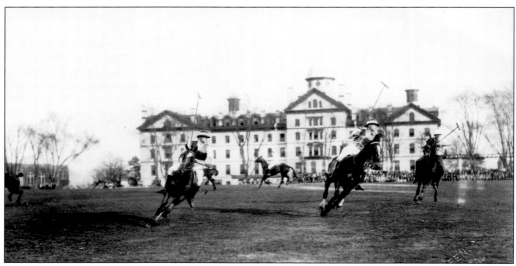

A Pennsylvania Military College polo match takes place in front of Old Main. (Widener Archives.)

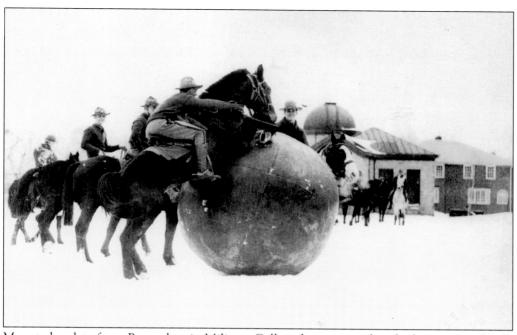

Mounted cadets from Pennsylvania Military College horse around with the giant pushball.
(Widener Archives.)

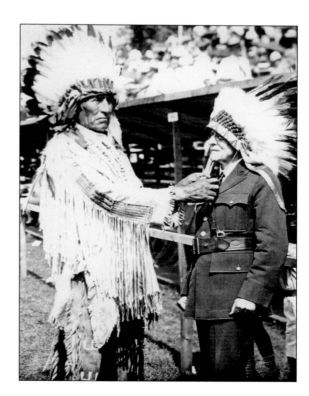

Red Tomahaw, a Sioux chief, presents
a war bonnet to Gen. Charles Hyatt,
head of Pennsylvania Military College,
in 1929.

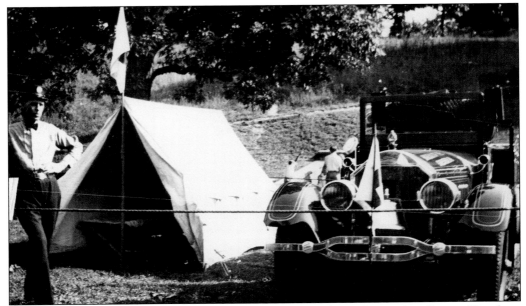

Camping in Chester Park was an activity for Chester residents. Pictured is George Hiorth, a fireman from Franklin Fire Company Squad No. 1. (Larry Scarpato.)

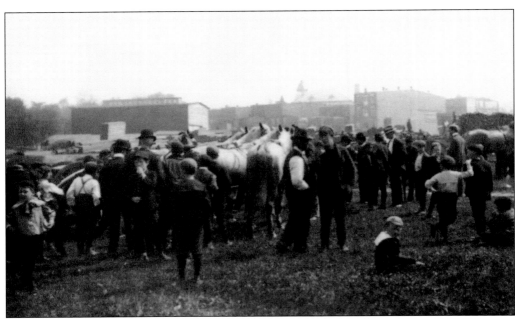

This photograph shows a rodeo that was held in Chester nearly 100 years ago. (DCHS.)

Eight

PLACES TO REMEMBER

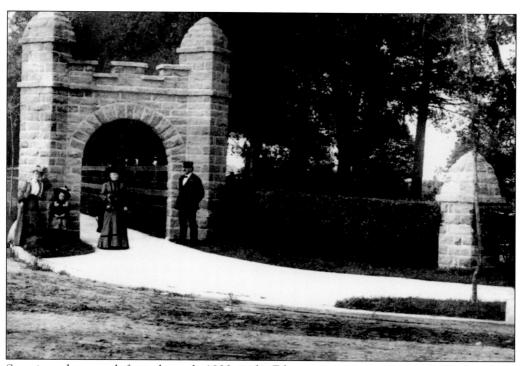

Seen in a photograph from the early 1900s is the Edgemont Avenue entrance to Chester Park. Emma Park, Joseph Park, Florence Park, and Martha Walley all prepare to stroll through the park on a summer's day. (DCHS.)

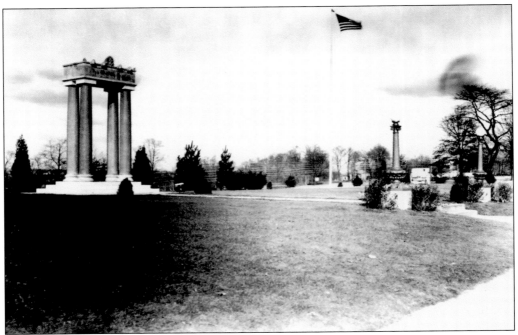

This 1937 view of Crozer Park shows the pillars at the Concord Avenue entrance that came from Chester National Bank. (DCHS.)

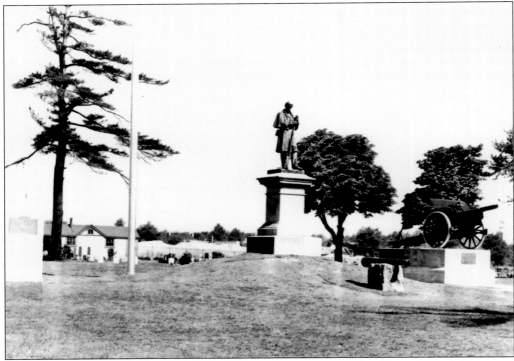

This photograph from 1932 shows the Civil War Memorial in the Chester Rural Cemetery. Many famous people are buried here. (DCHS.)

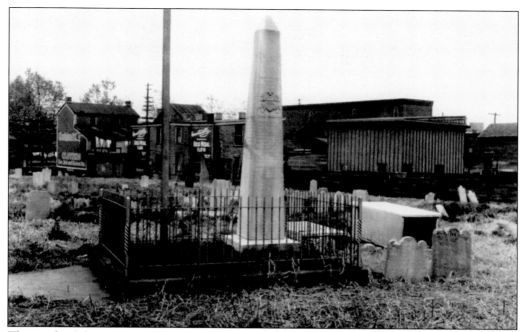

This is the John Morton grave site in Old Swedes Cemetery. He signed the Declaration of Independence in 1776. His vote broke the tie for the colonies to declare independence from England. (DCHS.)

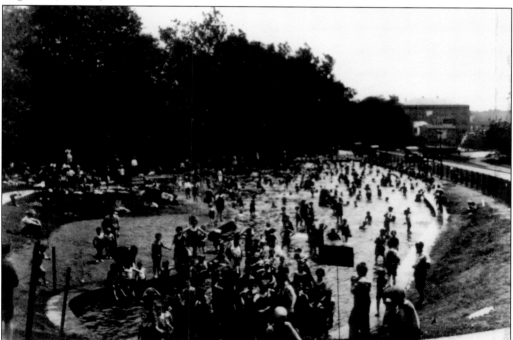

The wading pool at Deshong Park is shown here in 1927. Located off Deshong Boulevard at the back of the estate, the pool was a popular place for children and adults to cool off in the summer. (DCHS.)

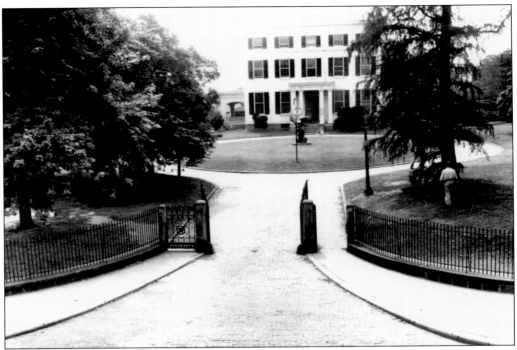

The Alfredo Deshong mansion, built in 1850 in the Italianate style, is pictured in 1949. Deshong gave his 23-acre estate to the people of Chester in 1913. Many rare plants grow on the grounds. (DCHS.)

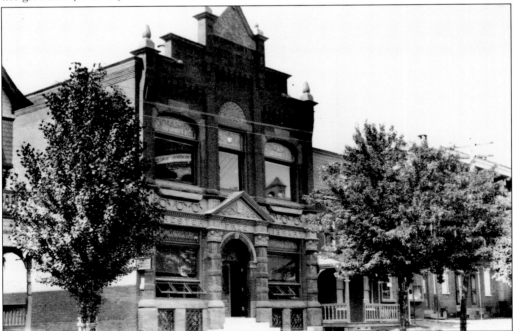

Chester Free Library, located on Ninth Street near Edgemont Avenue, became the J. Lewis Crozer Library when the original structure was demolished. (DCHS.)

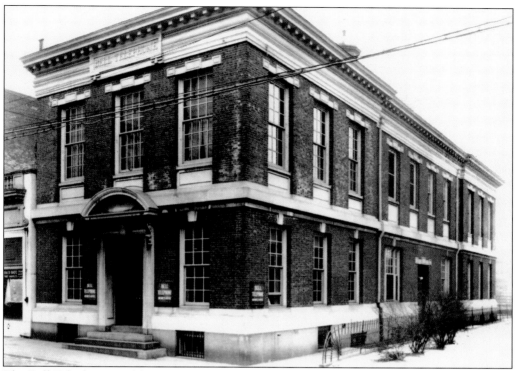

The Bell Telephone Building is shown in 1924. This was the first telephone exchange building in Chester. (DCHS.)

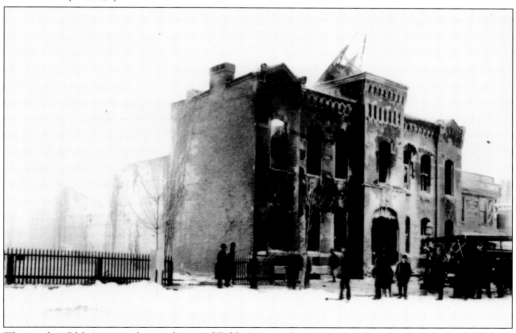

This is the Old Armory, located east of Fifth Street, the morning after the fire that gutted it in the 1920s. (DCHS.)

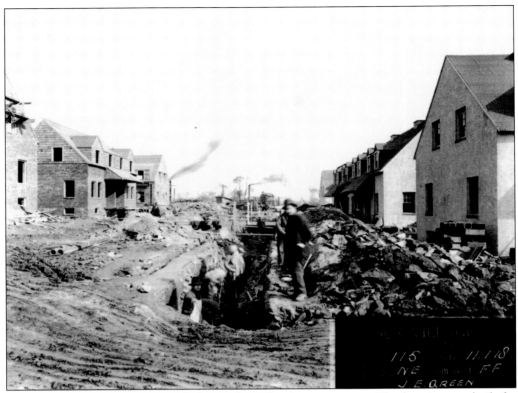

Sun Village men are seen at work during the village's construction. The housing was built for the men working for the Sun Shipbuilding Company. (DCHS.)

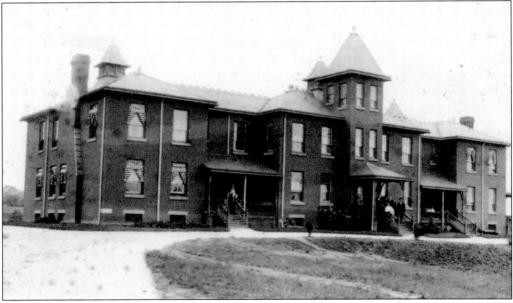

Chester Hospital is shown at its original location on Ninth Street. The new Chester High School was later built at this site. (DCHS.)

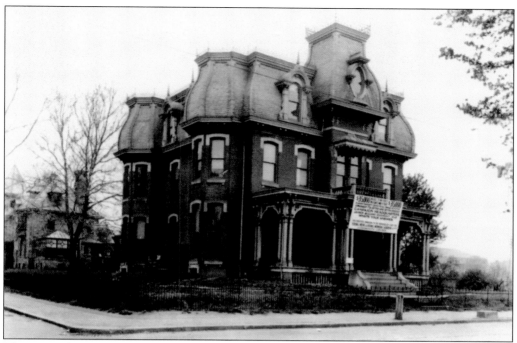

The J. Frank Black mansion, on Fourth Street, is shown in 1921. Black was a bank president, prominent citizen, and millionaire. (DCHS.)

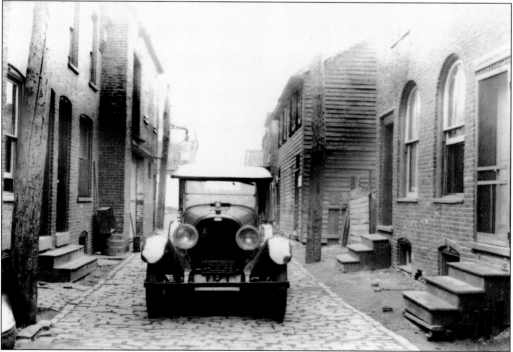

Bethel Court is seen in this c. 1920s photograph. The birthplace of Ethel Waters, this area of ill repute was known around the world, and many sailors stopped here. (DCHS.)

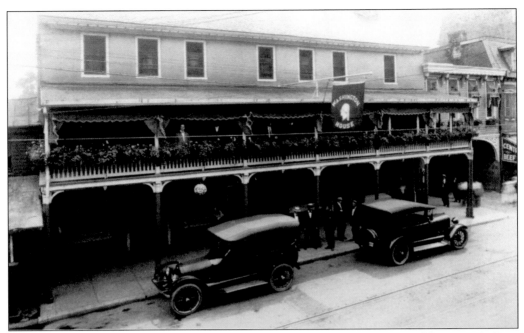

The Washington House was built in the 1750s. General Washington stayed here in 1777, at which time he wrote the only account of the defeat at the battle of the Brandywine. The house was demolished in the 1950s. (DCHS.)

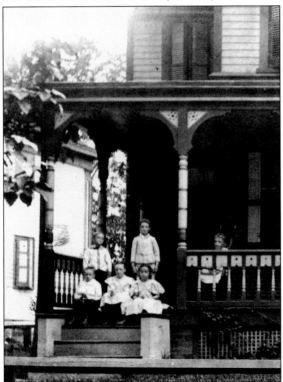

This view of 2220 Chestnut Street shows Chester Baker on the front porch as a child. He was born in this house in 1891. He preserved a great amount of Chester and Delaware County history. (DCHS.)

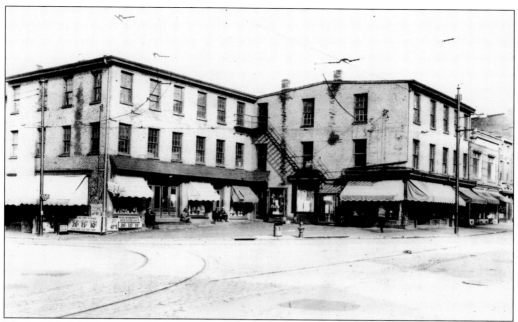

The Penn Building, which became the Broomall's department store, was a popular place to shop in the city. (DCHS.)

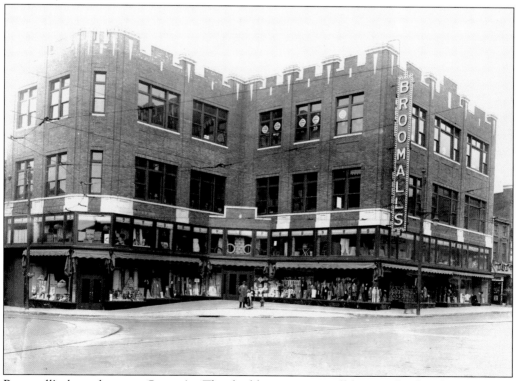

Broomall's later became Stotter's. The building was a well-known landmark in Market Square. (DCHS.)

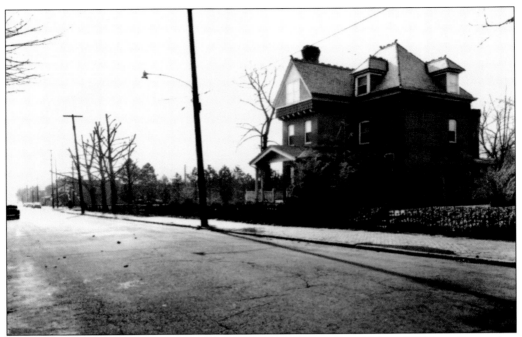

The home of William Provest Jr. is seen at its original location at 12th and Walnut Streets just before its demolition in 1960. Provest was a leading architect in Chester from 1870 through 1910. (DCHS.)

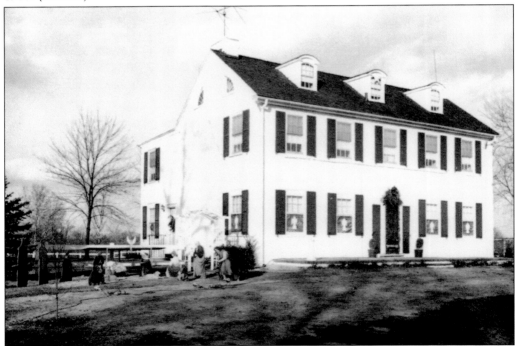

The Davis House in Chester Park is seen here in 1955. The house was built for Judge Hannum's daughter in 1835 and was demolished in the 1990s. (DCHS.)

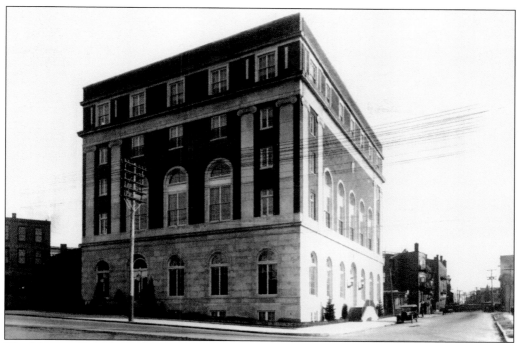

The Masonic Temple was built in 1920 at Ninth and Welsh Streets. This was a new home for the Masons. (DCHS.)

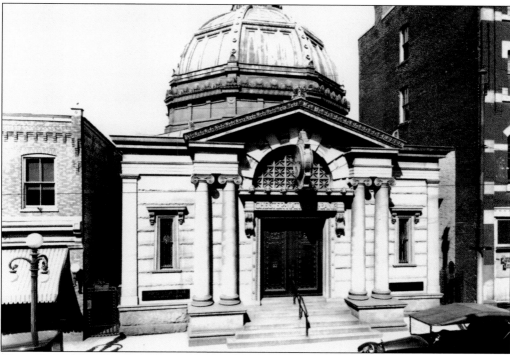

The pillars of the Chester National Bank's façade, seen here c. the 1920s, were used to make a monument in Crozer Park. (DCHS.)

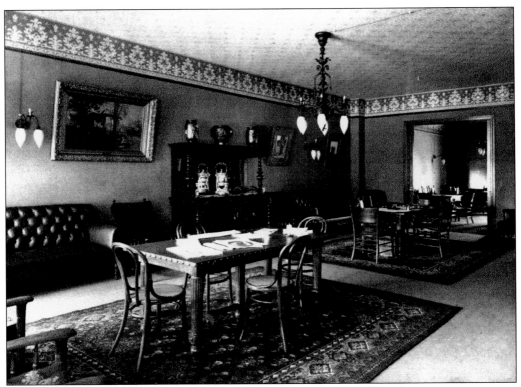

This photograph of the interior of the Penn Club was taken in 1898. This was a gentlemen's club where all of the leading men of the town relaxed. (DCHS.)

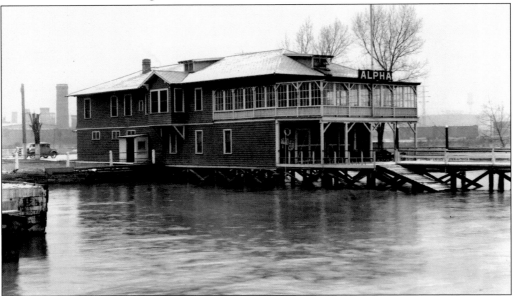

The Alpha Boat Club on the Delaware River was built in the late 19th century. It survived until the World War II–era expansion of the Sun Shipbuilding Company to produce Victory ships. (DCHS.)

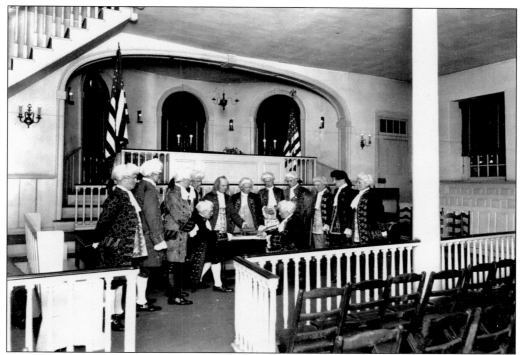

Shown is a reenactment of John Morton's 1766 oath of office as high sherrif of Chester County. The event was held in the 1724 Colonial Court House. (DCHS.)

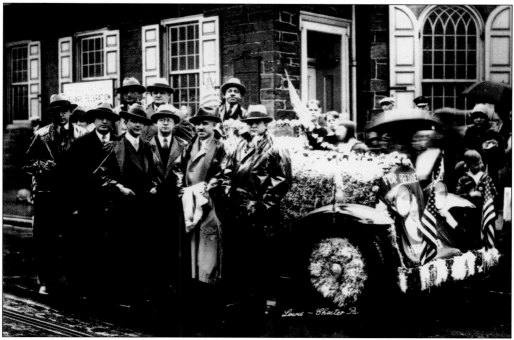

These people cannot be deterred by rain. They are campaigning for Herbert Hoover's run for president in front of the Colonial Court House. (DCHS.)

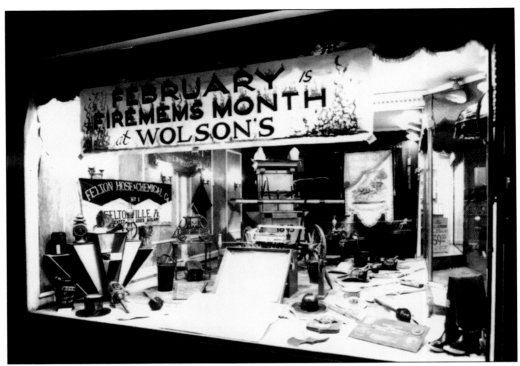

Wolson's held an annual Firemen's Month sale. The sign is misspelled, but the items in the window drew in customers. (DCHS.)

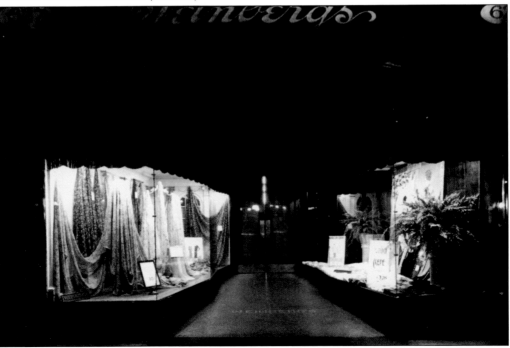

The Weinberg's storefront is seen at night in this photograph. (DCHS.)

Nine

A LOOK BACK

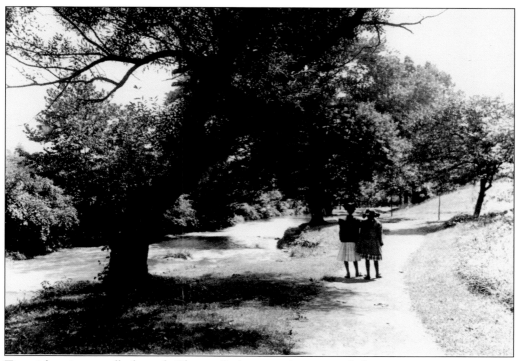

Two girls enjoy a walk through Chester Park on a quiet summer's day.

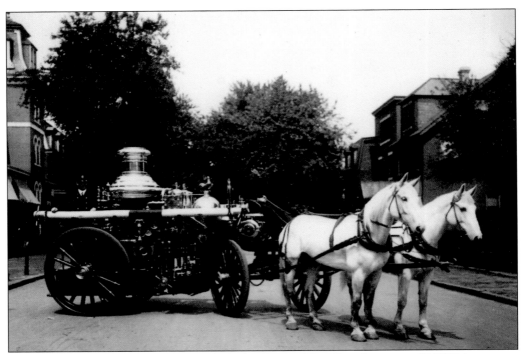

Seen is a double horse-drawn engine from the Hanley Hose Fire Company. (DCHS.)

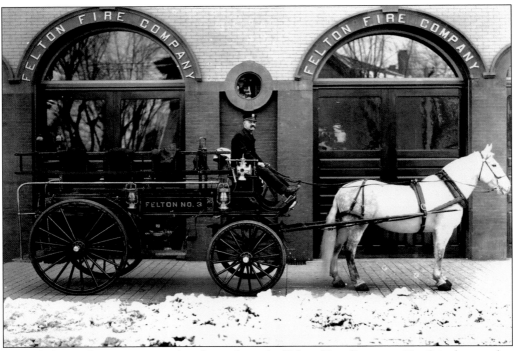

A single horse-drawn wagon with a driver from the Felton Fire Company No. 3 is shown after a snowfall. (DCHS.)

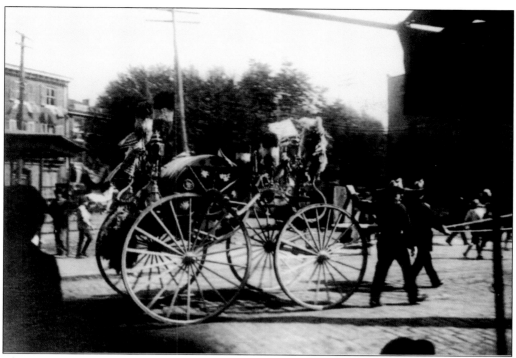

This view shows a fire engine from the 1800s in a parade through Chester. (DCHS.)

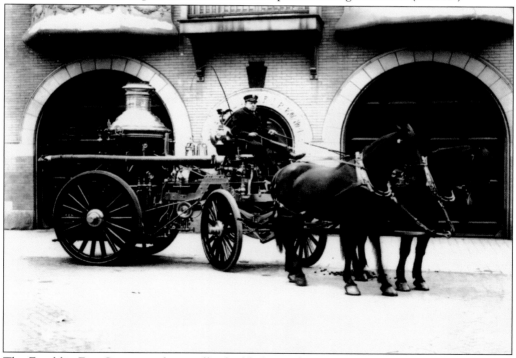

The Franklin Fire Company shows off a double horse-drawn engine with driver in front of the station. (DCHS.)

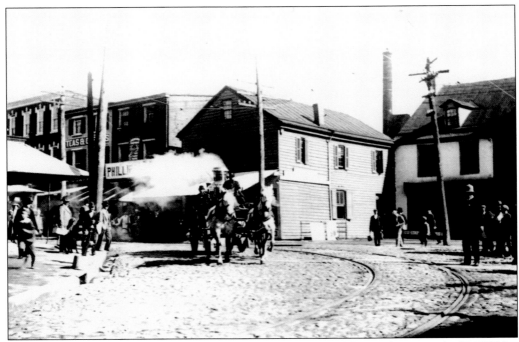

Firefighters respond to a fire on Market Street in a steam-fired, horse-drawn truck. (DCHS.)

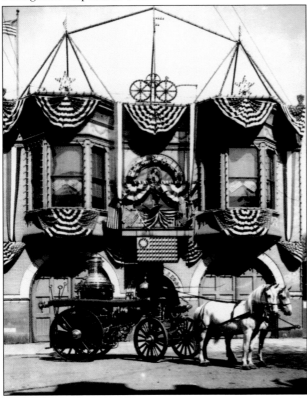

The Felton Fire Company is fully decorated for the holiday. (DCHS.)

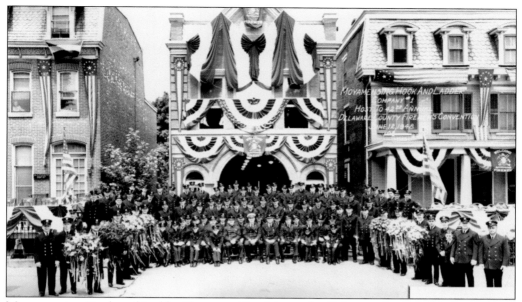

Moyamensing Hook and Ladder Company No. 1 hosts the Delaware County Fire Convention in 1948. (DCHS.)

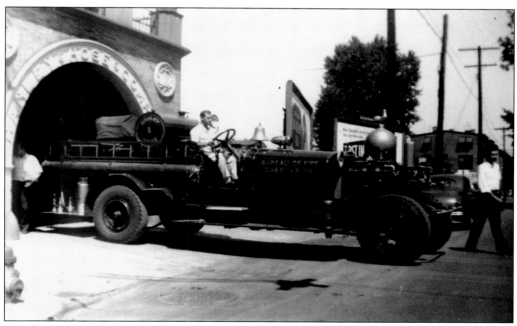

Members of the Hanley Hose Fire Company roll out their new pumper in 1939. (DCHS.)

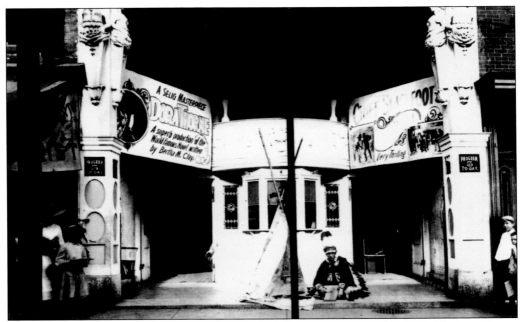

The Grand Theatre, located on Market Street, was the first 5¢ movie house in Chester. Here a Native American and his tepee are seen in front of the theater. (DCHS.)

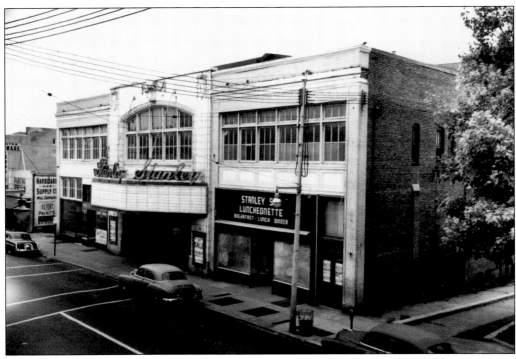

The Stanley Theatre was located on Edgemont Avenue in Center City. (DCHS.)

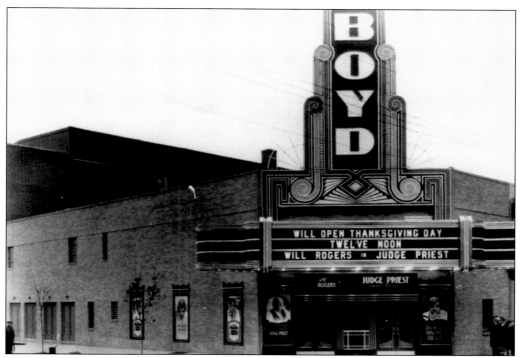

Showing on opening day at the Boyd Theatre are Will Rogers and Judge Priest in the movie *Twelve Noon*. (DCHS.)

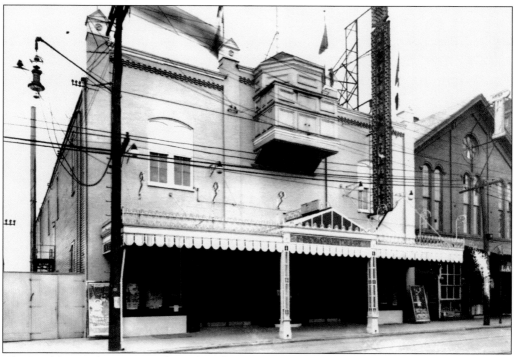

The Washburn Theatre, seen here, later became the State Theatre. (DCHS.)

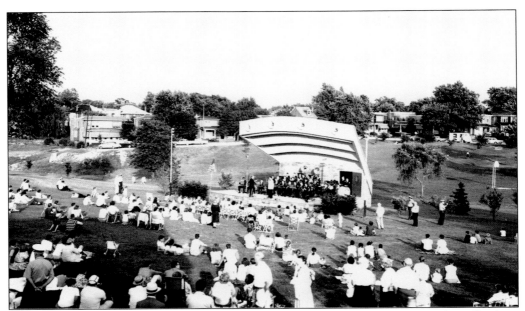

A concert is held on the lawn at the Chester Park band shell in the late 1950s. (Smedley.)

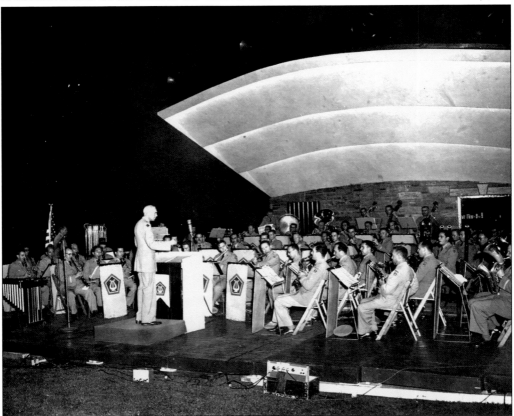

This photograph shows an evening concert at the Chester Park band shell. (Smedley.)

The Four Aces were a musical group from Chester. Their No. 1 hit song was "Three Coins in the Fountain." Al Alberts is at the top center. (Al Palagruto.)

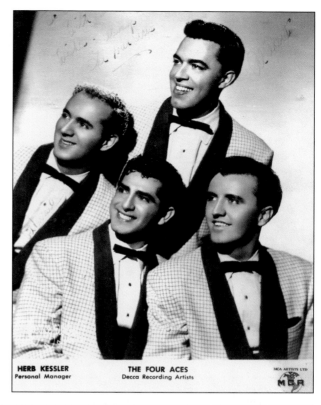

HERB KESSLER
Personal Manager

THE FOUR ACES
Decca Recording Artists

MCA ARTISTS LTD
MCA

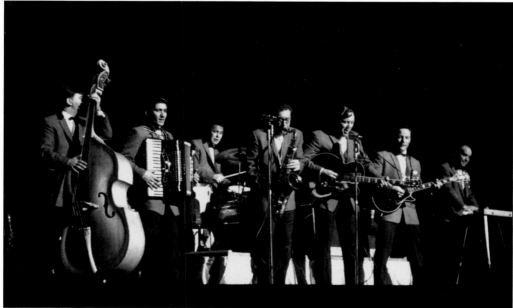

Bill Haley and the Comets were another musical group from Chester that originated rock-and-roll with their first hit song "Rock Around the Clock." Some residents may have noticed musical notes imbedded in the sidewalk while walking in Chester. (Lou Pulos.)

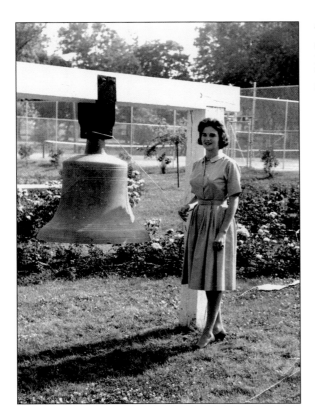

This photograph shows the USS *Chester* bell displayed in the Chester Park Rose garden in the 1950s. The ship was named for the city of Chester. (Smedley.)

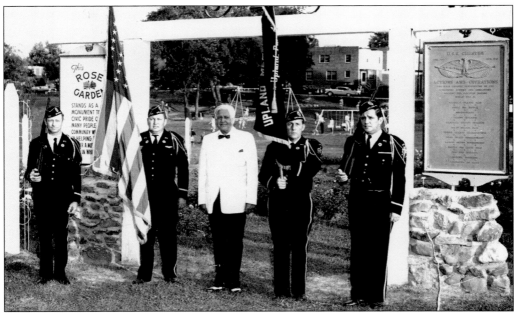

Clarence Smedley is pictured in a white suit with the local color guard at the USS *Chester* memorial in the Chester Park rose garden. The plaque tells of the ship's service history. (Smedley.)

This Halloween goblin in Chester Park is awaiting the start of a night of trick-or-treat. (Smedley.)

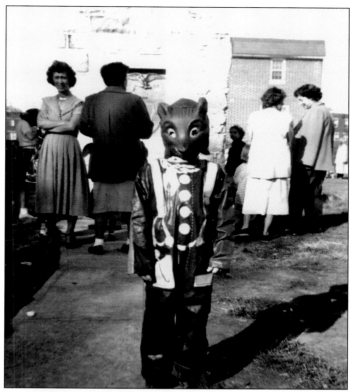

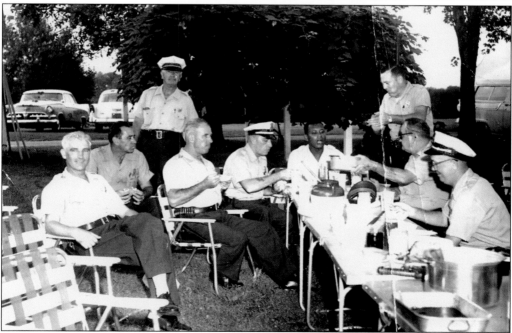

Chester's finest enjoy a Fourth of July picnic in Chester Park. A good time was had by all. (Smedley.)

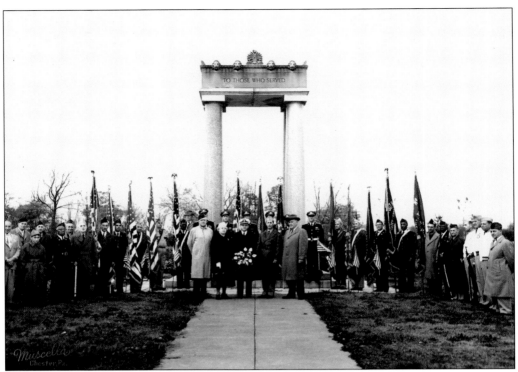

This photograph shows a special day honoring veterans in Crozer Park.

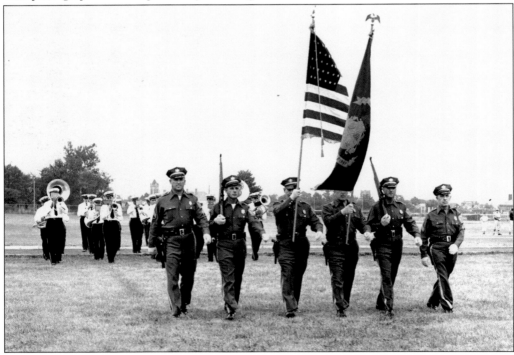

Members of the Chester Police Department are shown on parade.

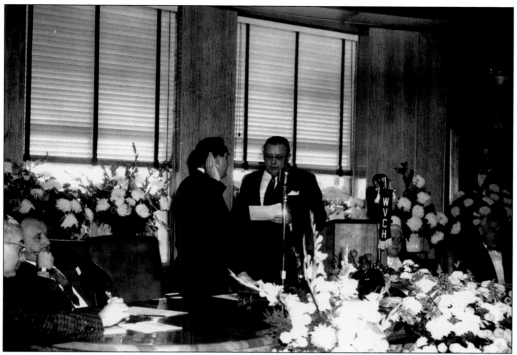

Mayor Eyre and Gorby are shown in 1960 in council chambers. (Smedley.)

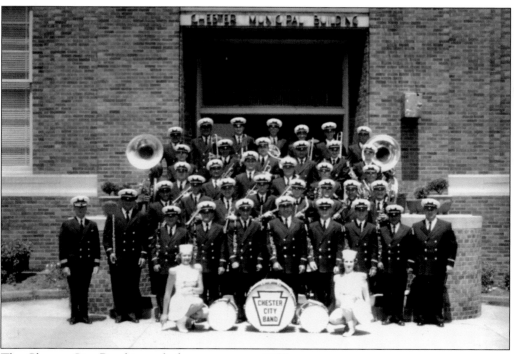

The Chester City Band is ready for a concert *c.* 1950.

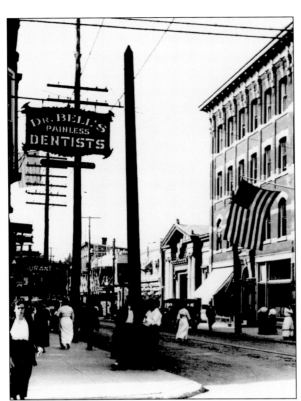

This photograph shows Dr. Bell's "painless" dentistry. (DCHS.)

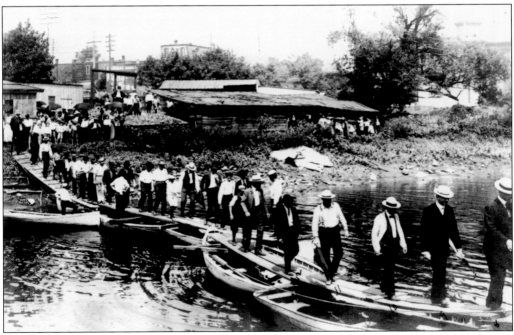

Inspection is being done on the construction of the Fifth Street Bridge across the Chester Creek. (DCHS.)

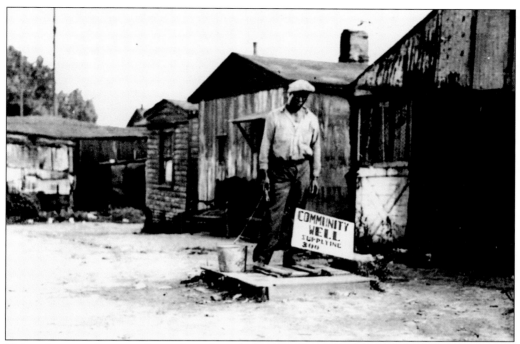

This photograph was obviously taken before indoor plumbing became the norm in Chester. (DCHS.)

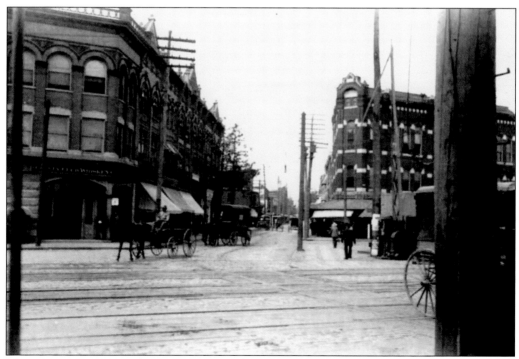

This 1890s street scene shows center city Chester before the automobile was in use. (DCHS.)

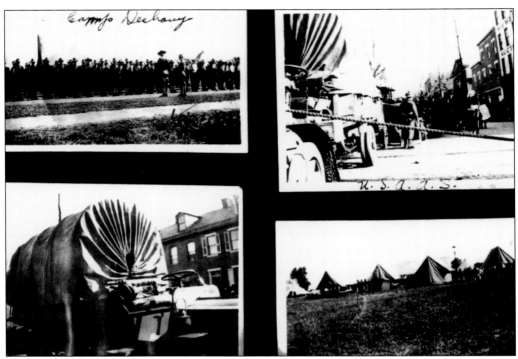

Soldiers are seen awaiting orders to ship out at the Camp Deshong Encampment in Deshong Park during World War I. (DCHS.)

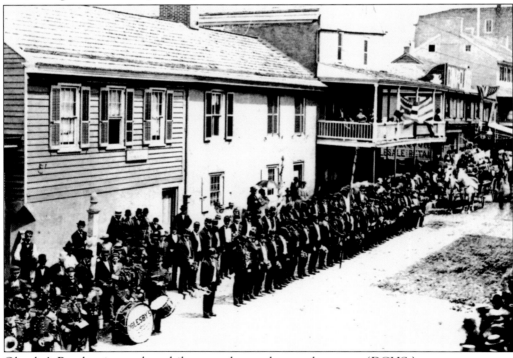

Olgesby's Band waits to play while a parade marches up the street. (DCHS.)

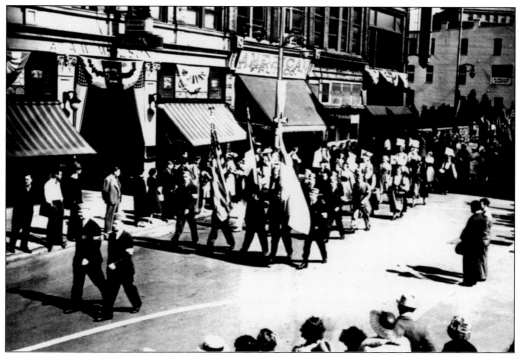

A Veterans Day parade marches through downtown Chester. (DCHS.)

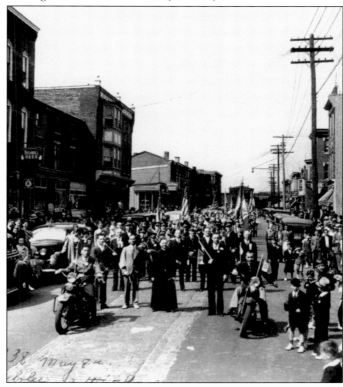

The silver jubilee of St. Anthony's in 1938 spills into the street as church members and neighbors celebrate. (DCHS.)

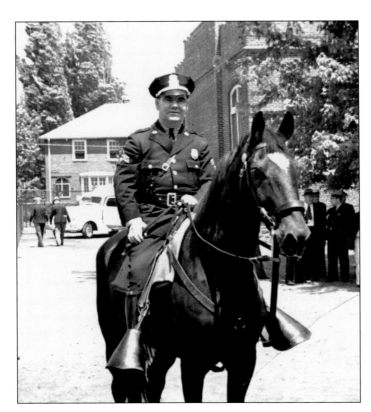

Officer Starr, a member of the Chester Police Department, is seen on his horse. (Eleanor Starr.)

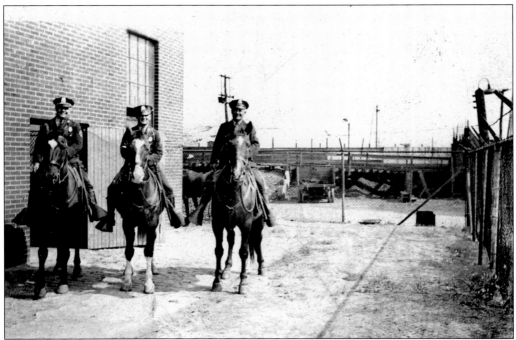

Three mounted Chester policemen begin their daily patrol of the city. (Eleanor Starr.)

This World War I Victory Day parade through Chester was held in honor of soldiers who gave their lives to defend the country.

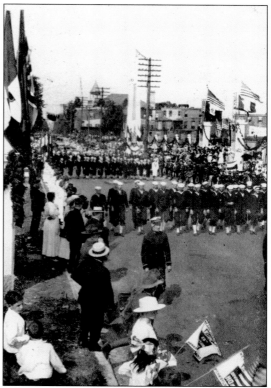

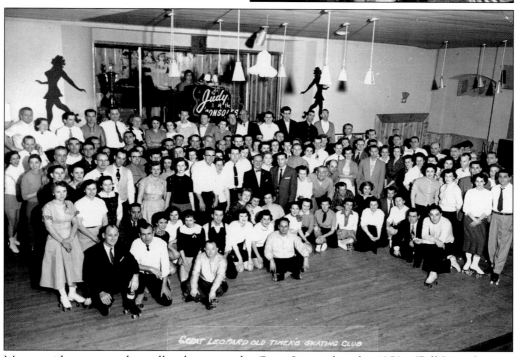

Many residents remember roller-skating at the Great Leopard in the 1950s. (Bill Jones.)

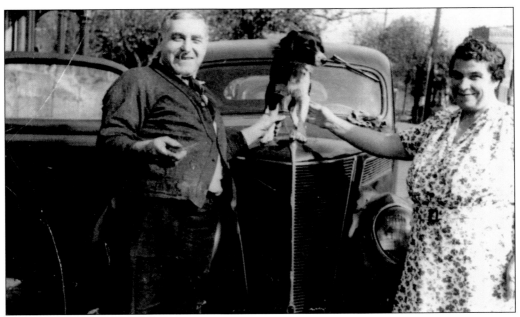

Pictured here are Chester residents Vera and Dennis Vermeychuk with their family pet.

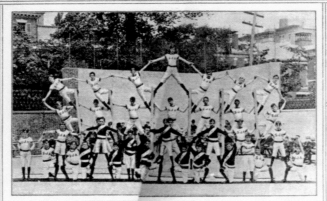

Musical and Gymnastical Entertainment

WILL BE HELD IN

THE GRAND OPERA HOUSE

Tuesday		Tuesday
Evening		Evening
June 7, '04		June 7, '04
8 P.M.		8 P.M.
Admission 25 cts.		Admission 25 cts.
Reserved Seats 35c and 50c		Reserved Seats 35c and 50c

By the Homeless Industrious Boys of St. Joseph's House

COR. EIGHTH AND PINE STREETS, PHILADELPHIA, PA.

For the Benefit of St. Michael's Holy Name Society

This poster advertises the Homeless Boys of St. Joseph's House performing for the benefit of St. Michael's Holy Name Society in Chester. (Dave Andrews.)

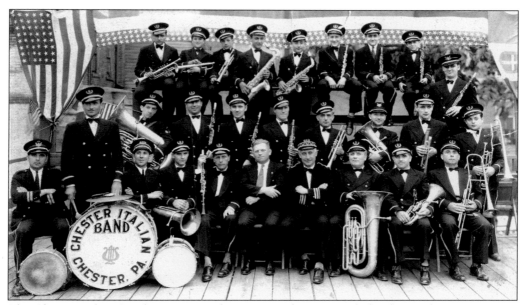

The Chester Italian Band prepares to play at an outdoor event. (Al Palagruto.)

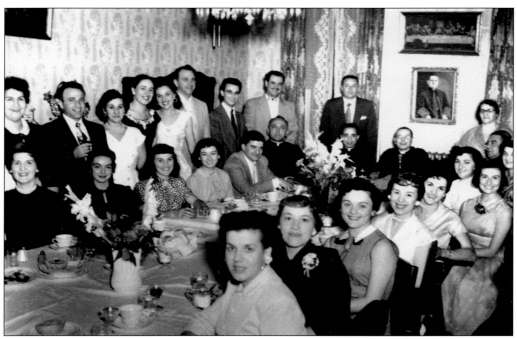

The St. Anthony's chorus takes time for a meal. One cannot help but wonder if they sang for their supper. (Al Palagruto.)

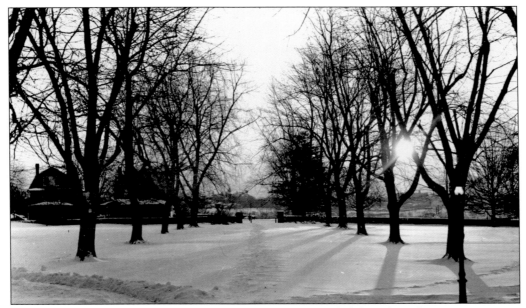

A winter day at the Crozer Seminary reminds us of the simple life and its pleasures.

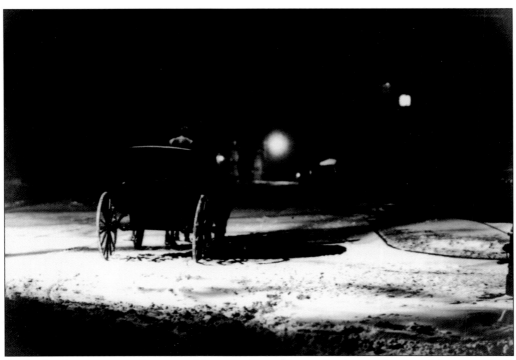

As the book comes to a close, we wish to thank you for purchasing our book and hope you look for other projects from the Chester Historical Preservation Committee.